MW00441956

THE UNOFFICIAL *Dollywood* COOKBOOK

THE UNOFFICIAL *Dollywood* COOKBOOK

From FRANNIE'S FAMOUS FRIED CHICKEN SANDWICHES to GRIST MILL CINNAMON BREAD, 100 Delicious Dollywood-Inspired Recipes!

Adams Media
New York • London • Toronto • Sydney • New Delhi

Adams Media
An Imprint of Simon & Schuster, Inc.
100 Technology Center Drive
Stoughton, Massachusetts 02072

First Adams Media hardcover edition
April 2023

Interior design and layout by Julia Jacintho and Michelle Kelly
Interior images © 123RF/emqan, tunejadez, Liubov Kotliar, Denys Holovatiuk, Zoia Nikolskaia, Nadejda Tchijova, Vasya Kobelev
Interior maps and illustrations by Artisticco, LLC
Photographs by Harper Point Photography
Photography chefs: Martine English and Christine Tarango

Manufactured in the United States of America

1 2023

Library of Congress Cataloging-in-Publication Data
Names: Browne, Erin K., author.
Title: The unofficial Dollywood cookbook / Erin K. Browne.
Description: First Adams Media hardcover edition. | Stoughton, Massachusetts: Adams Media, 2023 | Series: Unofficial cookbook | Includes index.
Identifiers: LCCN 2022035047 |
ISBN 9781507219966 (hc) |
ISBN 9781507219973 (ebook)
Subjects: LCSH: Cooking, American--Southern style. | Cooking--Tennessee--Pigeon Forge. | Amusement parks--Tennessee--Pigeon Forge. | Dollywood (Pigeon Forge, Tenn.) |
LCGFT: Cookbooks.
Classification: LCC TX715.2.S68 B7884 2023 |
DDC 641.59768/893--dc23/eng/20220803
LC record available at https://lccn.loc.gov/2022035047

ISBN 978-1-5072-1996-6
ISBN 978-1-5072-1997-3 (ebook)

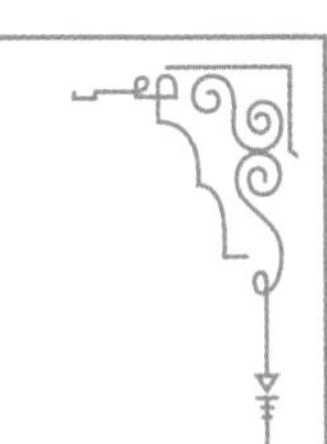

Acknowledgments

I guess I should start in the most obvious place, since this book would not have been completed without the help of my husband, Matt. During my months of writing, he shouldered the lion's share of the parenting during evenings and on weekends so that I could meet my deadlines. He never wavered in his confidence in me and was quick to offer advice, praise, and helpful critique.

I'm grateful for my kids, Jasper and Shelby, who showed support and excitement for this project even at such young ages. I'll never forget serving frozen pizza for dinner one tired evening and hearing from my youngest, "You should put this in your cookbook, Mommy!" I love you, kids.

Thank you to my parents, Jim and Cathy Kendrick, for doing everything they could to get the book in as many hands as possible and for always being two of my biggest cheerleaders. And another thank you to my mother-in-law and father-in-law, Diane and David Browne, who whisked the kids away on many fun weekends so I could nab some extra time in the kitchen or in front of my laptop.

I cannot express enough appreciation for my best friends, Kara and Remington Brown, who are a pillar of support in my life and have always been there to celebrate the good and commiserate over the bad.

I also want to extend a deep, heartfelt thank you to Julia Jacques and the entire team at Adams Media who believed in me enough to offer this incredible opportunity and make me a published author. Finally, to my agent, Joe Perry, my advocate and ally, who walked me through my first foray into the publishing world and made it such an enjoyable process. I couldn't have done it without you!

Contents

CHAPTER FOUR

Lunch in the Foothills...73

CHAPTER FIVE

Dinner with Dolly...97

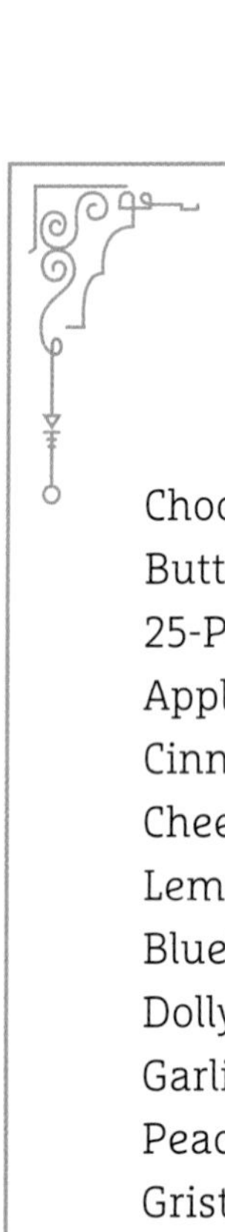

CHAPTER SEVEN

Lovin' from the Oven...147

CHAPTER EIGHT

Country Candy and Ice Cream...181

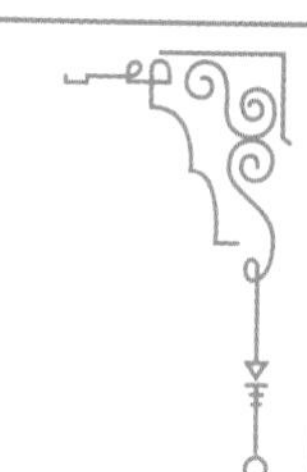

Preface

For more than a decade, I've been blogging recipes and sharing fun foodie finds. During this process, I realized that the recipes I am most attached to are those inspired by something personal to me, be it a family recipe from my childhood, a historical snack highlighted in a period drama I've watched, or a really great meal consumed on one of our family trips. Using my experiences and interests to create, photograph, and share recipes has become my way of expressing my excitement for them.

I have been fortunate to live my entire life in East Tennessee, so Dollywood has been a sanctuary for my family, and we visit as often as we can. We know the park layout by heart, and my kids thrive on putting together a specific itinerary for riding our favorite rides and indulging in our favorite foods. When I was given the opportunity to create a collection of recipes re-creating iconic dishes served on Dollywood properties, I could not have been more passionate about the project. After lots of squealing and happy-dancing after receiving the news, of ***course*** I had to start planning extra trips to Dollywood for research...and for fun! My kitchen and office became littered with early drafts of recipes, and my fridge and freezer were overflowing with the results of endless trials. It was a labor of love, and I'm so grateful to be able to share this special collection with you.

My hope is that when you try these recipes at home, they will not only fill your belly with some amazing food; they will also fill your heart with memories of your trips to Dollywood—or get you excited about visiting for the first time. Indulge in a Lumber Jack Pizza and hear the deafening whistle of the Dollywood Express. Bite into a Butterfly Pretzel and feel the wind on your face from the Wild Eagle roller coaster. Each time you choose a recipe from this book and gather your ingredients, the spirit of Dollywood will be manifested right inside of your home.

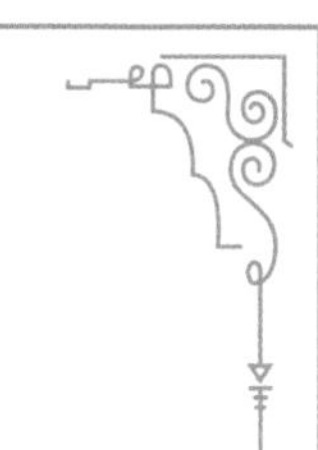

Introduction

Nestled in the foothills of the Great Smoky Mountains of East Tennessee—just behind the lively parkway of Pigeon Forge—is a special theme park where the griddles are hot and the vittles are hearty. Inside the gates of Dollywood, life moves more slowly, enveloping you in a warm hug of Southern hospitality and down-home cookin'.

In *The Unofficial Dollywood Cookbook*, you'll become acquainted with all things edible in Dollywood and its sister attractions. In Part 1, you'll be given a brief history, a tour of the food options in nine sections of the main park, notable choices at Dolly's nearby venues, and an overview of the specialized menus available during Dollywood's ever-rotating schedule of themed festivals throughout the year. Next, you'll learn some invaluable tips to assist you while working in the kitchen, as well as gain an overview of recommended tools and equipment.

Part 2 is where the fun really kicks off, presenting one hundred delicious recipes evocative of the culinary offerings at Dollywood's flagship theme park and beyond. This collection includes everything you need to create a special snack, sweet treat, or full-blown Southern meal. These nostalgic delights are presented with user-friendly techniques and step-by-step instructions so you can re-create the soul-stirring essence of the park anytime, right in your own kitchen. There's something for every occasion, including:

- **Southern comfort meals and sides,** like Dolly's favorite Meatloaf Stackers, Granny Ogle's Pinto Beans, perfect BBQ Pork Sandwiches, and, of course, Southern Buttermilk Biscuits.

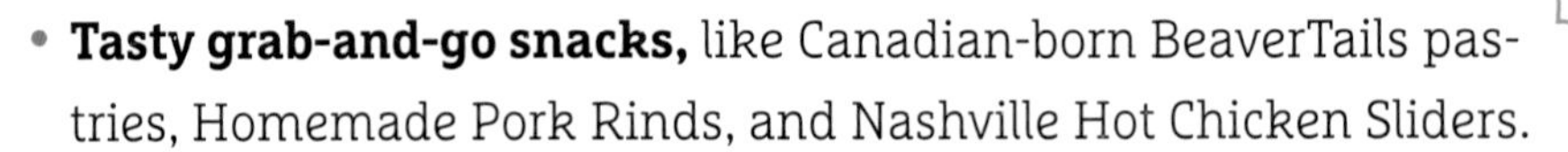

- **Tasty grab-and-go snacks,** like Canadian-born BeaverTails pastries, Homemade Pork Rinds, and Nashville Hot Chicken Sliders.
- **Dollywood's iconic treats,** such as the famous Grist Mill Cinnamon Bread, 25-Pound Apple Pie, and Red Velvet Funnel Cakes.
- **Inspired signature cocktails,** slushies, teas, and more, like the Honey Sage Lemon Drop, Frozen Strawberry Lemonade, and Dolly's must-have Sweet Tea.

Dollywood's official motto is "Love Every Moment," and it's guaranteed that you'll do just that as you pull on your boots, crank up some bluegrass, and make something tasty. Have fun!

PART ONE
A Heritage of Food

Dollywood has come a looong way from its inception in 1986, when it started as a singular theme park less than half the size it is now. The attraction has grown to an empire consisting of several properties operating under the Dollywood umbrella. But there is one thing that has remained consistent from the start: the dedication to making and serving fantastic food reminiscent of the cherished memories Dolly Parton has growing up with her large family in East Tennessee.

In this part, you'll explore a brief history of Dollywood, from how it started to how it has blossomed into the successful park it is today. Then you'll delve into the themed areas in the main park and the yummy food options available in each, from the restaurants that have been pillars of Dollywood since day one to the newer options and more creative cuisine enjoyed during seasonal festivals. Next, you'll take a look at the eats and treats you can find at Dollywood's neighboring attractions, because the foodie fun doesn't stop outside the walls of the original property. After all of that, you'll probably be dying to try some of this goodness for yourself, but before you skip ahead and dig into the recipes, make sure to read through Chapter 2 for some invaluable tips and recommended equipment to set you up for success in the kitchen.

CHAPTER ONE

Very Culinary: An Overview of Dollywood Food

Dollywood is an authority on Smoky Mountain food, and it takes quite the army to make the delicious victuals sold every single day between March and January. In an average season, Dollywood produces a mind-blowing 212,250 loaves of cinnamon bread, 48,000 pounds of pork rinds, 614,000 pounds of popcorn, over 160,000 hot dogs and corn dogs, more than 170,000 pizzas, and over 87,000 funnel cakes! That's a lot of ingredients, a big ol' labor of love, and just a very small portion of what is available in the park. This chapter will explore each area of the park in detail, from the theme and attractions of that location to the dishes and sips on the menus. You'll also discover the themes, rides, and tasty offerings in the outlying Dollywood properties, including the water park, dinner show attraction, and Dolly's four-star resort.

Dollywood

As of 2022, Dollywood is a sprawling 150-acre amusement park that hosts nearly three million guests every season. Heart-stopping rides, top-notch performances, stunning landscapes, and, of course, heaps of mouthwatering food and drinks make it quite the family retreat. But before the success of the park as it is known today, Dollywood came from humble beginnings (just like Dolly herself), existing as three attractions before Dolly Parton ever came on board.

In 1961, the park opened as Rebel Railroad, designed around the coal-fired steam engine now known as the Dollywood Express. Rebel Railroad had a general store, a blacksmith, and an old-fashioned saloon. In 1970, the park saw big changes when it was purchased by Art Modell, the owner of the Cleveland Browns. Modell changed the park to a Wild West theme and added mock robberies to the train ride, a log flume ride, and the Robert F. Thomas Chapel that is still standing today. Then, in 1976, brothers Jack and Pete Herschend purchased the park and changed its name to Silver Dollar City. A goal of the remodeled park was to show off the craftsmanship of local leather smiths, blacksmiths, wood-carvers, and soap makers. It was during this time that the grist mill—the first of its kind in Tennessee in over one hundred years—was built. (This mill would later became the production center of Dollywood's famous cinnamon bread, the most popular treat sold at the park today.)

Silver Dollar City saw more success than the two previous versions of the park, and in the early 1980s, the Herschend brothers reached out to Dolly Parton and suggested a partnership. On May 3, 1986, the brand-new park opened under the Dollywood name and welcomed 1.3 million people in its first season—more than double the number of visitors that Silver Dollar City saw the year before.

Though the reborn Dollywood opened with a number of food establishments, including the current Granny Ogle's Ham 'n' Beans and an earlier version of Aunt Granny's Restaurant—Aunt Granny's Dixie Fixin's—the new park underestimated the popularity it would see, and, as a result, one of Dollywood's earliest food-themed stories was born. The charming story surrounds something that can commonly be found in a school lunch box: a bologna sandwich! Since the park was inundated with so many guests, the food lines grew to outrageous wait times—two hours or more—prompting the staff to start making bologna sandwiches to hand out to the guests to keep them fed. Needless to say, park managers got to work in the off-season, adding several new restaurants and other amenities before the gates opened again the next year.

Today, Dollywood is an indomitable force of food, consisting of long-established theme park snacks, blue-ribbon Southern cuisine, and creative seasonal and international fare. The modern-day park consists of eleven themed areas, nine of which house the sundry food operations that make Dollywood a culinary mecca. Let's explore them!

Rivertown Junction

When the park opened under its current name in 1986, Rivertown Junction was one of the original areas that survived the many upgrades over the years. There, you can tour the replica of Dolly Parton's childhood mountain home, marvel at the distinctive Harvey Water Clock, do some home decor shopping, and feed the fish and ducks while strolling around and enjoying the water and fountains. If you don't mind getting wet, you can experience the thrill of the Smoky Mountain River Rampage for an exciting white water rafting adventure.

It is impossible to miss the Market Square BIG SKILLET® pavilion as you cross into Rivertown Junction. If it isn't the aroma of sizzling steak, sausage, peppers, and onions that grabs your attention, it's the sight of the absolutely massive trademarked skillets used to cook everything up. The menu here is constantly updated with new options celebrating the current festival. Rivertown Junction is also where you can find some of the more classic theme park snacks like salty-sweet kettle corn popped right in front of you at Country Cookers or a deep-fried funnel cake at Crossroads Funnel Cakes topped with syrups, candy, fresh fruit, whipped cream, and more. When lunchtime rolls around, indulge in a footlong corn dog from Dogs N Taters, served with Dollywood's signature seasoned Tater Twirls. If you're ready to sit down to a full spread, bring your appetite to Aunt Granny's Restaurant. The establishment serves an unmatched selection of entrées like fried chicken and catfish; sides including macaroni and cheese, mashed potatoes, and hot biscuits; and tantalizing desserts like fruit cobbler and key lime pie.

The Village

The star attraction of The Village, which opened in 1986, is the Dollywood Express Train Depot, where guests can board an authentic 110-ton steam engine and embark on a twenty-minute, 5-mile ride through the park and surrounding foothills. Two locomotives—nicknamed Klondike Katie (built in 1943) and Cinderella (built in 1938)—are rotated in and out of operation. Other attractions include retail shopping, performance venues, and Dollywood's beautiful Village Carousel featuring sixty painted animals, including one lead horse with a long blonde mane that is known, of course, as "Dolly."

Iron Horse Pizza—formerly Victoria's Pizza—is the main restaurant in The Village. The shop serves flatbread pizzas, fresh salad, and other snacks. The covered patio is an ideal place to relax and watch the train come and go. If you're just cruising through, PaPaw's Roadside Market provides packaged snacks, cotton candy, and ice cream for some fast nibbles.

Craftsman's Valley

Demonstrations by local craftspeople were a major theme of the former Silver Dollar City park, and that spirit stayed alive with the opening of Craftsman's Valley in 1986. Here, you are treated to talented artists, wood-carvers, blacksmiths, leather smiths, and candlemakers crafting their wares (which can be purchased in the nearby shops). This area houses some of Dollywood's top thrill rides and attractions like Blazing Fury, Daredevil Falls, and the hair-blowing Tennessee Tornado roller coaster. If you're looking for a stage performance that doesn't involve singing and dancing, the Wings of America Birds of Prey show offers an up-close look at the impressive avian creatures that call Dollywood their sanctuary and home.

The shining star of Craftsman's Valley food is the warm cinnamon bread available from the Grist Mill, the bestselling treat in all of Dollywood that is considered to be the number one "must eat" item in the park. If smoked meats are more your jam, you're in luck, since there are various options for chowing down on hot pit ham, turkey legs with meat that falls off the bone, and award-winning pulled pork barbecue sandwiches. You can also find just about any side dish that's ever graced a Southern mama's Sunday supper table. Sit-down restaurants include Granny Ogle's Ham 'n' Beans and Miss Lillian's Smokehouse, while there are more casual options with outdoor seating like Hickory House BBQ and Miss Lillian's BBQ Corner. Crunch into some cracklin' hot pork rinds made on the spot at the aptly named Pork Rinds stand, or pick up some quick snacks to stash in your bag at Mr. Jerry's Sit-N-Sip Refreshments.

Showstreet

The Showstreet area of Dollywood opened in 1992. The main entrance to the park was moved there from Rivertown Junction, making Showstreet the first place that guests see when they enter the park, laying their eyes on the beautiful facade of the Showstreet Palace Theater. Dolly's inspiration for Showstreet came from her love of all of the glitz and glamour of the showbiz industry.

Showstreet is home to Front Porch Café, a full-service restaurant that offers some of Dolly's favorite Southern meals and notable desserts in a comforting down-home atmosphere. Spotlight Bakery also calls Showstreet home and is where you can find Dollywood's famous 25-Pound Apple Pie, as well as an impressive display case full of freshly baked pastries, muffins, and cookies. If that's not enough to satisfy your sweet tooth, stop by the Sweet Shoppe Candy Kitchen for a variety of homemade candies such as taffy, fudge, truffles, and candy apples. Or take home a jar of the Smokies with a locally made product from the Southern Pantry, a specialty grocer where you can pick up packaged kitchen ingredients like jams and jellies, dressings, mixes, and canned produce. To beat the heat, Showstreet Ice Cream blends and scoops everything from old-fashioned soda floats and milkshakes to hand-dipped ice cream and waffle bowl sundaes. For snacks on the go, the walk-up stands—Showstreet Snacks and Showstreet Frozen Lemonade—sell some of the park's classic treats, like Buttered Popcorn, Butterfly Pretzels, and Cinnamon-Glazed Nuts.

Country Fair

Walking through Dollywood's Country Fair is like time traveling to an old-timey carnival complete with classic games and timeless rides. When the area first opened in 1993, it even had a Ferris wheel that has since been removed. Now Country Fair is full of fun rides like the Amazing Flying Elephants, Lemon Twist, the Scrambler, and more. There are plenty of thrills for the grown-ups and older kids as well as adorable kiddie rides for the park's youngest visitors.

No carnival trip is complete without some nibbles, and the focal point of the culinary offerings in Country Fair is Grandstand Café. Here you can find Frannie's Famous Fried Chicken Sandwiches and other fair favorites like chicken tenders, hot dogs, seasoned fries, and nachos. Ready for a brain freeze? Grab a cone swirled high with soft serve ice cream from Blue Ribbon Cones. For more casual snacking, pick up a soft drink and some pillowy cotton candy from the open-air Midway Market stand.

Jukebox Junction

Jukebox Junction opened its streets in 1995 and is a nostalgic place themed after 1950s Sevierville, Tennessee. The area has an entirely different feel from the surrounding sections of the park and is punctuated by painted streets, old-fashioned vehicles, and vintage storefronts. Here, you can drive miniature versions of classic cars on one of the area's most popular rides— Rockin' Roadway—while music from the fifties blasts through the speakers. If it's an adrenalin rush you're after, head to the Lightning Rod, a hybrid wood and steel roller coaster themed after a 1950s hot rod and featuring a stomach-flipping 165-foot drop and a top speed of 73 mph. For something a little more low-key, take in a show at the Pines Theater or do some shopping at the Hi-Octane souvenir shop.

When you're ready to nosh, set your sights on the shiny red and silver building of Red's Drive-In, a classic diner modeled after the former Red's Café in downtown Sevierville. Dolly reportedly had her very first hamburger at Red's following a dentist appointment as a child. Dollywood's reimagined diner serves retro classics like burgers, fries, and an ever-changing selection of thick and creamy milkshakes. With quick service and ample outdoor and indoor seating, Red's is an easy place to stop for lunch in a fun setting during a visit to the park.

Adventures in Imagination

Learn all about Dolly Parton's personal history and her rise to fame by moseying over to Adventures in Imagination. This $10 million expansion opened in 2002 and is home to the Chasing Rainbows museum, which is an immersive experience detailing Dolly's life and professional career through a collection of stories and memorabilia. Out in front of the museum you can step inside Dolly's retired tour bus to get a glimpse of what life on the road was like for the country music star. Catch a show at the Dreamsong Theater and wrap up your visit with some shopping in Dolly's Closet.

Timber Canyon

The rustic decor and wooded landscape of Timber Canyon—unveiled in 2006— illustrate Dollywood's nod to the logging communities of the Smoky Mountains. The theme is carried through the attractions themselves, like the monstrous Thunderhead roller coaster—a wooden structure set between the hills that features a harrowing 100-foot drop. You can also take an expedition through an abandoned coal mine on the Mystery Mine steel coaster that'll send you into darkness along the 1,811-foot track. The Canyon is known by seasoned visitors as a pleasant, tree-covered "secret path" accessible directly from the main entrance for those who want to skip the busier Showstreet area after entering the park.

Lumber Jack's Pizza is the primary food joint in Timber Canyon, and what better way to fuel a marathon of riding roller coasters than with pizza? The quick-service counter serves up personal pan pizzas with popular toppings like pepperoni and cheese and rotates through more creatively topped pizzas depending on the current season.

Wilderness Pass

Tucked away in the far north corner of the park, Wilderness Pass opened in 2008. The area has two nationally recognized roller coasters: Wild Eagle and FireChaser Express. FireChaser is unique in that it propels riders forward and backward, making it the country's first dual-launch coaster. Wild Eagle—identified by the imposing statue of a bald eagle at its entrance—is the longest roller coaster in the park. It is also the nation's first wing-style coaster (appropriate, isn't it?) that has the car situated beside the track rather than above or below it. If you have the kiddos in tow, don't worry, because Wilderness Pass also has giant building block and water play areas to keep them busy while the grown folks fulfill their need for speed. On your way through, make sure to take in the beautiful Plaza at Wilderness Pass, an outdoor entertainment venue where you can gawk at a 50-foot animated Christmas tree during the Smoky Mountain Christmas festival or a 40-foot-tall pile of larger-than-life jack-o'-lanterns that light up the night during the Harvest Festival.

The bulk of the options for nibbles in Wilderness Pass are snack stands such as Splinter's Funnel Cakes, SkyView Snacks, and The Dog House. A 2021 update to the area brought in local business from outside the gates with the addition of a food truck park. The food trucks operate on a rotating schedule that can be found online or on Dollywood's mobile app. Guests can try scratch-made local doughnuts, authentic gyros and other Greek fare, tacos, and meatball subs.

Owens Farm

Tucked away in its own little corner of the park, Owens Farm opened to the public in 2011. The charming little area is named for Dolly's mother's family as well as the vice president of marketing and public relations at Dollywood, Pete Owens. Visitors can't miss the classic red barn that serves as the entrance to Owens Farm's main attraction: Barnstormer. The ride is designed to mimic a flight on a post-World War I aircraft when pilots bought surplus airplanes and charged people a quarter in exchange for a ride. The farm also offers two play areas for Dollywood's youngest guests: Granny's Garden and Lil' Pilots Playground. The play areas offer structures of low height and smooth materials that are perfect for little ones to enjoy.

Wildwood Grove

The year 2019 saw the opening of the largest expansion in Dollywood history: Wildwood Grove. The $37 million project brought with it new attractions, rides both gravity-defying and gentle, a restaurant, food stands, and a 4,000-square-foot indoor play area for children. Wildwood Grove's theme is the most fantastical of any other area in the park and was inspired by Dolly Parton's childhood daydreams, evident by the towering mythical Wildwood Tree that comes to life with 650 multicolored butterflies that light up among the tree's 9,000 leaves.

Wildwood Grove also injected some brand-new cuisine into the park's already impressive repertoire with the introduction of Till & Harvest, a counter service eatery with covered patio seating that puts a Southern sparkle onto Mexican cuisine. Create your meal with customizable entrées like burritos, bowls, and salads piled high with your choice of meats, cheeses, and classic Mexican toppings like fresh salsa, onions, and sour cream. Adjacent to the restaurant is Sweets and Treats, a quick-grab stand offering small bites like maple-flavored popcorn chicken and tater tots or sweet delights like Benjamin Bear's Brownies and churro sundaes.

Festivals

Throughout the year, Dollywood hosts some of the biggest festivals in the region. The seasonal celebrations are marked by overhauling the park with awe-inspiring decor and new live entertainment, and expanding existing menus with interesting dishes featuring new flavors and unique regional and international dishes well beyond Dollywood's well-established reputation for expert Southern cuisine. Starting at the beginning in springtime and rotating through until winter, the festivals as of the 2022 season are Dollywood's Flower & Food Festival, Smoky Mountain Summer Celebration, Harvest Festival, and Smoky Mountain Christmas. You can visit Dollywood's website or mobile app to stay in the know about the most up-to-date festival schedule.

Dolly Parton's Stampede

Dolly's unique dinner show opened in 1987 under the name of Dixie Stampede. The name was changed to Dolly Parton's Stampede in 2018. The 35,000-square-foot arena puts on a spellbinding show featuring horse riding and special effects while guests dine on an elaborate four-course feast. The dinner starts with Stampede's famous Creamy Vegetable Soup with a hot buttermilk biscuit for dunking. Next, a plate piled high with a whole rotisserie chicken, smoked pork loin, fire-roasted vegetables with rice and quinoa, corn on the cob, and a seasoned half-potato is served. For dessert, a warm and flaky apple turnover finishes off the evening. The feast is designed to be eaten without silverware—even the soup is sipped from a bowl with a handle—though cutlery is provided on request.

Dollywood's Splash Country

Dollywood grew by one more full-blown park in 2001 when Splash Country opened its doors. The 35-acre water park has something for both thrill-seekers and pool loungers. You can spend a chill afternoon at the lagoon-style Cascades pool, float down the 1,500-foot lazy river on the Downbound Float Trip, or fly down the 280-foot high-speed slides of Fire Tower Falls. Dollywood's sister park doesn't slouch in the food department either and has plenty of available poolside eats. Warm lunch items like hot dogs and burgers with loaded fries, burrito bowls, pizza, chicken tenders, and Nashville Hot Chicken Sliders are on offer as well as cooler items for hot days like fresh salads, sandwiches, and fruit cups. Satisfy a sweet craving at Berries N Cream and enjoy hand-dipped or soft serve ice cream cones and ice cream sandwiches, or try their namesake, Berries 'n Cream—a layered dessert of soft serve ice cream and chilled fruit compote. Splash Country's most unique offering comes straight from Canada—BeaverTails—a deep-fried whole-wheat pastry finished with a plethora of sweet toppings.

Dollywood's DreamMore Resort & Spa

Opening on July 27, 2015, DreamMore Resort & Spa continued Dolly's lifelong passion for resonant storytelling and the importance of family fellowship with its aim to be a welcoming mountain retreat that upholds the same standard of warm and fuzzy treatment as any of Dolly's endeavors. Dining options at the resort are rooted by Song & Hearth: A Southern Eatery, which serves family-style and buffet breakfast, Sunday brunch, and dinner in a homey sit-down restaurant. The meals include favorites like Dolly's Stone Soup, shrimp and grits, and dry-rubbed pork ribs. The impressive dessert buffet features a literal doughnut wall: a wooden board with old-fashioned doughnuts hanging from pegs, waiting to be plucked off and consumed. While Dollywood itself is a dry park, you can celebrate at the resort with a libation from the restaurant's innovative list of cocktails.

Next Steps

Now that you're an expert on all of the bites and gulps of Dollywood, you're probably itching to plan a trip to East Tennessee to try some of this stuff for yourself. But lucky you, you'll get to re-create some of the exemplary dishes in Dollywood's line-up without packing a suitcase. Keep reading to arm yourself with the knowledge needed to approach the recipes in this book with confidence. It's almost time for the dinner bell!

CHAPTER TWO

Helpful Tips for the Southern Cook

You're one step closer to Dollywood-flavored deliciousness! But first, let's make sure that you're equipped with all the information and tools you'll need for success in your tasty pursuits. In the pages ahead, you'll learn some essential cooking and baking tips as well as possible pitfalls and how to avoid them. You'll also find a guide to the tools and equipment that are used in the recipes in this book. By the end of this chapter, you'll be ready to stock up on ingredients, grab your mixing bowls, and churn out some amazing Dollywood creations!

Essential Cooking and Baking Tips

The following are helpful tips for avoiding common issues that can arise in the kitchen.

Read the Recipe

Before diving into a recipe, make sure to read it from top to bottom. Gather all the needed equipment, check that you have all the required ingredients, and ensure that you understand each step of the instructions. Take note of how long you anticipate the entire recipe to take, including prep, so that you can manage your time efficiently and have everything ready to go when you need to serve your dish. Sometimes it is helpful to do all the prep work at once, like washing and chopping vegetables and premeasuring ingredients, so that you don't get distracted by rummaging around in your pantry or refrigerator.

Don't Walk Away

Don't stray too far from the kitchen when you're smack-dab in the middle of a recipe, especially if it's the first time you're making a dish. Vegetables burn, batter gets overmixed, chicken dries out, or a number of other unsavory mishaps occur when you let your attention drift. In baseball, they say to keep your eye on the ball, and the same advice applies here: Keep your eye on the stove!

Measure Flour Correctly

Baking is an exact science, so measuring ingredients properly is crucial. When measuring flour, never dip the measuring cup directly into the bin. Doing so will pack the flour into the cup, you'll end up with more than you need for the recipe, and your baked goods will be dry or crumbly. Measure flour by spooning it into the measuring cup until it is slightly mounded above the rim, then use a butter knife or similar straight edge to level off the top. You can apply this technique when measuring most dry ingredients except for those that are to be measured "packed," like brown sugar.

Be Gentle

Once flour is added to a recipe, working or mixing the dough encourages gluten development. While this is a good thing when making yeasted bread dough for Grist Mill Cinnamon Bread or Butterfly Pretzels, overmixing or overworking the dough is detrimental to more fragile baked goods like Southern Buttermilk Biscuits or Blueberry Muffins. If you are creating a pastry that incorporates cold butter into the dough, working it too much will soften the butter, and the result won't be as tender or flaky as it should be.

Taste and Adjust

Dried and ground herbs and spices vary in potency depending on the brand and how long they've been sitting on a pantry shelf. While specific amounts for seasonings are given for every recipe, you should also taste your creations at various points during the cooking process to determine if additional flavor is needed. Add extra seasonings in very small amounts—a tiny pinch at a time—and taste after each addition until deliciously perfect. Just remember to play it safe and never taste raw meat, eggs, or other ingredients that are not meant to be consumed uncooked.

Use Quality Ingredients

The quality of any of the ingredients you use in a recipe makes a major difference in how the final dish tastes. Choose fruits that are ripe and juicy, vegetables that were harvested at peak time, and high-quality herbs and spices that are not expired. Speaking of expired, don't forget to check the expiration date of leavening agents like baking soda, baking powder, and yeast, as using expired versions of any of those can really flatten (literally) your baking attempts.

Know Your Oven

Not all ovens are created equal! An oven that runs hotter or cooler than the temperature it is set to will wreak havoc on your baked recipes. Think cookies and cakes that are burnt on the outside and still raw on the inside or oven-fried chicken that just won't crisp up. Use an oven thermometer to calibrate your appliance and make sure it is heating to the proper temperature. Also be aware of any "hot spots" and rotate pans regularly to ensure even baking.

Adjust Cook and Bake Times

The cook and bake times given in these recipes are close guidelines, but they are not set in stone. To allow for differences in home appliances, always use your instincts when following the instructions. Is your ground beef still a bit pink at the end of the recommended time? Cook it an extra few minutes. Is your soup or sauce not thickening up? Dressing not set in the center? Be patient, it'll get there. Always keep an eye on things and don't be afraid to pull things off the heat sooner or later than the exact time that the recipe states.

Helpful Tools and Equipment

The following are all of the tools you'll need to start making some edible Dollywood magic in your kitchen. The tools are listed alphabetically for easy reference whenever needed.

Bakeware

Several standard baking pans are used for the recipes that call for oven baking. Opt for light metal pans over glass or dark metal for optimal heat transfer. You'll need: 18" × 13" (medium) and 9" × 13" (large) baking sheets, loaf pans, a large roasting pan, a jumbo muffin pan, a 9" × 13" cake pan, a 9" springform pan, an 8" × 8" square pan, and a deep 10" × 15" lasagna pan.

Blender

A high-powered blender is a game changer for creating the smooth frozen beverages and milkshakes found in Chapter 9. A 64-ounce pitcher is a good standard size when making several servings at once.

Bowls

A variety of sizes of mixing bowls—small, medium, and large—is helpful when combining ingredients or making dough. Have at least one glass or microwave-safe bowl on hand to easily melt butter or chocolate. Several shallow containers—any material—with wide bottoms are useful for dipping and dredging when deep-frying.

Cast Iron Skillet

This is a key piece of equipment that Southern cooks absolutely need to have in their kitchen. A seasoned cast iron skillet—one that has layers of oil baked on to create a nonstick surface—is amazing for shallow frying, sautéing, and creating crispy crusts on cornbread. You'll also use a cast iron skillet for making Dollywood's signature 25-Pound Apple Pie! Both an 8" and a 10" skillet are needed for those recipes.

Cocktail Shaker

A standard stainless steel cocktail shaker is needed for superbly shaken beverages, whether using alcohol or not. You can use a Cobbler, Boston, or French shaker—whichever you prefer.

Cutting Board

There are many recipes in this collection that require chopping up fruits, vegetables, and other ingredients. A sturdy wooden cutting board acts as a shock absorber when chopping and also preserves the sharpness of knives.

Food Processor

A food processor makes quick work of chopping nuts or other solid ingredients as well as puréeing fruits and vegetables. If you don't have a food processor, you can use a blender instead.

Measuring Cups and Spoons

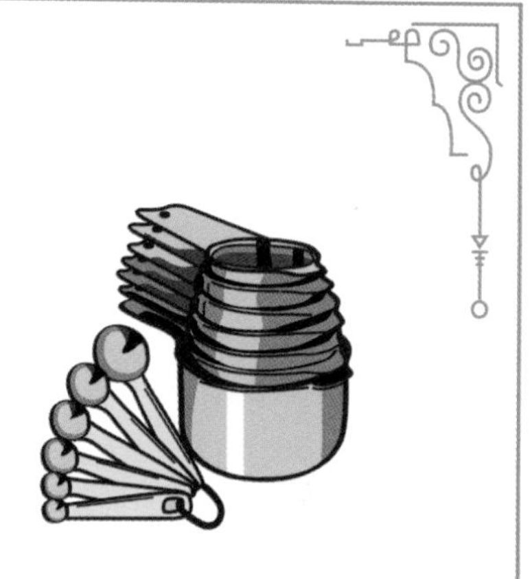

You will need a full set of measuring spoons ranging from 1/8 teaspoon to 1 tablespoon. You'll also need a set of measuring cups ranging from 1/4 cup to 1 cup. Glass measuring cups with a pour spout are wonderful for precise measuring of liquids.

Metal Rack

For most of the fried dishes in this book, an oven method is included for those who prefer baking to deep-frying. Using an oven-safe metal rack placed over a baking sheet allows air to circulate all around the food, preventing the soggy bottoms common in oven-fried recipes. While the breading will never get quite as crunchy as when it is fried in oil, this easy trick will help achieve a tasty result.

Mixer

For all recipes that call for an electric mixer, a stand or hand mixer can be used. The dough hook attachment on a stand mixer makes kneading bread dough an easy task, though you can also knead by hand. If you don't have any kind of a mixer, grab a sturdy whisk and put some elbow grease into it—that's what old-fashioned Southern cooks used to do, after all!

Paper, Plastic, and Foil

Lining baking sheets with parchment paper prevents sticking and makes for easier cleanup. Foil is helpful for preventing too much browning during extended times in the oven. Plastic wrap is useful for covering dough before letting it rise, for tenderizing meat, and for other uses. Gallon-sized zip-top bags are perfect for brining and marinating. Smaller plastic bags make melting chocolate for drizzling a simple process.

Piping Bags and Tips

Large piping bags with a ½" closed star tip will create perfect churro shapes with deep grooves that are made for packing on flavorful toppings. A ½" open star tip is great for swirling whipped cream onto individual servings of Dolly's Banana Pudding.

Pizza Stone

While you can bake pizzas on a large baking sheet just fine, a good pizza stone will elevate them to something special, with a perfect, crispy crust and evenly heated toppings.

Popsicle Molds and Sticks

You'll need some basic six-cavity Popsicle molds—silicone works best—to make Fruit Paletas in Chapter 8. You will also need some Popsicle sticks, long wooden skewers, and lollipop sticks for making all of the various "treats on a stick" found in this collection.

Ramekins

You will need four 6-ounce ceramic ramekins for shaping homemade waffle bowls and baking molten lava cakes. If you don't have any in your kitchen, a jumbo muffin pan can be used instead.

Silicone Mat

While a silicone mat isn't required, it is very helpful. A large mat provides a nonstick surface for kneading dough, rolling out pastry crusts, shaping candies, and more. Most mats have rulers and other useful size markers on them to make sure your creations are the proper dimensions.

Slow Cooker

A 7-quart slow cooker is where the magic happens when making Dollywood's award-winning pulled pork.

Spiralizer

A spiralizer attachment for a stand mixer or a stand-alone spiralizer with varying blade sizes will allow you to replicate Dollywood's signature Tater Twirls seasoned fried potatoes.

Stovetop Cookware

Stainless steel pots with heavy bottoms, handles, and lids are useful when making sauces and soups. You'll need a mixture of small, medium, and large sizes. A wide sauté pan has many uses and is great for sautéing and simmering while also being perfect for deep-frying with its taller vertical sides (a large stockpot can also be used). A large enameled Dutch oven is perfect for tender pot roast.

Strainers

You will need a traditional colander for draining pasta and vegetables in the sink. A fine-mesh strainer is great for dusting confectioners' sugar as well as straining out lumps in pudding to achieve a silky, smooth texture.

Thermometer

A thermometer is required for close monitoring of the temperature of frying oil or cooked candies. Choose a style that clips onto the side of the pan—these are usually labeled as a candy or deep-fry thermometer. An instant-read digital thermometer can also be used for frying and is ideal for testing the internal temperature of meat and fish.

Utensils

An array of utensils and small hand tools are helpful for whipping up Dollywood goodness. A few things to have at the ready include sharp chef knives, large and small solid and slotted spatulas, wooden spoons, nonstick silicone spatulas, rolling pin, wheel-style pizza cutter, cheese grater, potato masher, whisk, soup ladle, pastry cutter, mandolin, meat tenderizer, and a set of metal tongs.

Waffle Iron

A Belgian waffle iron is needed to create Liege Waffle Ice Cream Sandwiches in Chapter 8. You can use an electric waffle iron or a stove-top iron—both will make delicious waffles. Be sure to follow the manufacturer's instructions for your individual iron. For Waffle Bowl Sundaes in Chapter 8, a specialized waffle cone maker is ideal for getting a pretty pattern, though you can use your oven if you don't have one.

Let's Get Cooking!

Now that you have the techniques and tools for mixing up some home cookin' there's just one more thing to do: Grab one final tool—your favorite apron—because it's time to get into the kitchen and have some fun!

PART TWO

Recipes from the Heart

Now that you know a little more about Dollywood, as well as the tips and equipment for whipping up Smoky Mountain magic in your own kitchen, it's time to get this shindig started! In this part, you'll discover one hundred recipes that replicate favorite menu items from Dollywood and its sister attractions. The recipes are organized by type and course so that you can easily find something to get your tummy rumblin'. Under each recipe title is the location where the original dish/drink is sold in the park. (Or has been sold in the past: Because Dollywood is constantly keeping things fresh, some of the items may come and go from the menus over the years.) So, barring any recent changes, the next time you take a trip to the Smoky Mountains you'll be able to try a few of these recipes for yourself. If a recipe was inspired by a limited-edition offering during one of Dollywood's annual festivals, the name of the festival and location in the park where it was sold are included in the recipe. You'll also be treated to some fun bits of trivia about Dollywood and Dolly Parton herself, the history of certain dishes, and serving suggestions so you can create a close copy of how the food is presented in the park.

Although these recipes were designed and developed to re-create the experience of kicking back at Dollywood, you can also use them as starting points to ignite your own creativity in the kitchen. Change up the flavors; add your own flair; and, above all, have fun!

CHAPTER THREE

Smoky Mountain Snacks

Do you love classic theme park eats like funnel cakes, kettle corn, and soft pretzels? Dollywood does it up right with all of those irresistible treats and more, and this chapter is where you'll learn to make them for yourself. Whether you've been to Dollywood one time, a hundred times, or haven't visited just yet, each time you make a recipe from this chapter, you'll be transported right to the mountains of East Tennessee. From staple snacks that are available all season long to fun flavors offered during the rotating festival schedule, these dishes are total people pleasers. You can try one at a time or make a day of it and create a whole spread of amusement park delights. Now, turn the page and get to snackin'!

Cinnamon-Glazed Nuts

Showstreet Snacks, Showstreet

Is there a more quintessential theme park treat than a paper cone filled with sweet, glazed nuts? Luckily, you can get your hands on these not long after entering the park gates, at the Showstreet Snacks stand—just follow your nose! The sweet aroma of cinnamon sugar is hard to miss (and resist). This version of cinnamon-glazed nuts mixes together the almonds, pecans, and cashews, but you can either separate them or use only your favorite for the whole recipe.

MAKES 3 CUPS

- 1 large egg white
- 1 teaspoon ground cinnamon
- ½ cup granulated sugar
- ½ cup packed light brown sugar
- ¾ teaspoon salt
- 1 teaspoon pure vanilla extract
- ⅛ teaspoon pure almond extract
- 2 tablespoons water
- 1 cup unsalted whole cashews
- 1 cup unsalted whole almonds
- 1 cup unsalted pecan halves

1. Preheat oven to 250°F. Line a large rimmed baking sheet with aluminum foil lightly sprayed with nonstick cooking spray.
2. In a large bowl, add egg white and use a hand mixer to beat until foamy. Add cinnamon, granulated sugar, brown sugar, salt, vanilla extract, almond extract, and water. Mix on medium-low speed, scraping sides of bowl as needed, until fully combined.
3. Add cashews, almonds, and pecans to bowl. Stir until fully coated. Spread onto prepared baking sheet and use a nonstick spatula to scrape bowl and get all of the coating onto nuts.
4. Bake on center rack 1 hour, stirring well every 15 minutes. Cool 1 hour before serving.

Buttered Popcorn

Showstreet Snacks, Showstreet

You can find Dollywood's bright yellow buttery popcorn at several food stands throughout the park, but if you want to get your hands on some as soon as you get through the gate, you can head on over to Showstreet Snacks right across from Dolly Parton's Celebrity Theater. Or skip the wait and enjoy a big batch at home!

MAKES 8 CUPS

2 tablespoons canola oil
¼ cup popcorn kernels
2 tablespoons clarified butter (ghee), melted
3 drops yellow food coloring
½ teaspoon popcorn salt

1. In a 4-quart heavy-bottomed pot over medium-high heat, add oil and four kernels of popcorn. Place lid on pot.
2. Listen closely, and when you hear all four kernels pop, lift lid and add remaining kernels. Replace lid and shake pot for 5 seconds.
3. When kernels begin to pop, shake pot for 5 seconds. As popping increases in speed, shake pot continuously.
4. When popping slows to 3 seconds between pops, remove from heat and transfer popcorn to a large bowl.
5. In a small bowl, add butter and food coloring. Stir to combine. Pour half of butter mixture onto popcorn and sprinkle on half of popcorn salt. Toss, then add remaining butter mixture and salt. Toss once more and serve.

Cooking Tip

You can make your own popcorn salt by adding table salt to a blender or coffee grinder and grinding it to a fine powder. The finer grains will adhere to popcorn better so that your snack is perfectly and evenly salted.

Fruity Pebbles Funnel Cakes

Crossroads Funnel Cakes, Rivertown Junction

Dollywood serves up many funnel cake toppings, ranging from a dusting of confectioners' sugar to strawberries and whipped cream, hot fudge, vanilla glaze, cinnamon sugar, or Reese's Peanut Butter. If you want even more tantalizing choices, the hosts at Crossroads offer a rotating menu of other seasonal or festival-themed options. This colorful Fruity Pebbles version was introduced to the menu in 2019 and quickly became a visitor favorite!

SERVES 3

¾ cup whole milk
1 large egg
½ teaspoon pure vanilla extract
1 tablespoon granulated sugar
½ teaspoon baking powder
⅛ teaspoon salt
1 cup all-purpose flour
1 cup Fruity Pebbles cereal, divided
4 cups canola oil
3 tablespoons confectioners' sugar
1 cup whipped cream
3 tablespoons colorful sprinkles

1. In a small bowl, whisk together milk, egg, and vanilla. In a medium bowl, stir together granulated sugar, baking powder, salt, and flour.
2. Add wet ingredients to dry ingredients, mixing until batter is smooth and free of lumps. Fold in ½ cup cereal.
3. In a wide sauté pan fitted with a thermometer, add oil 1½" deep and set over medium heat. Heat oil to 375°F.
4. Fill a squeeze bottle or funnel (with a ½" opening) with batter. Drizzle batter into hot oil in a swirling motion, beginning in the center and building up the base of the cake, then working your way out.
5. Fry batter 2 minutes or until golden on the bottom. Use tongs to carefully flip funnel cake and fry an additional 45 seconds or until golden. Transfer to a large plate lined with paper towels to drain. Repeat frying process with remaining batter.
6. Top funnel cakes with a light dusting of confectioners' sugar, remaining ½ cup cereal, whipped cream, and sprinkles. Serve.

Change It Up

Leave the Fruity Pebbles out of the batter to create a classic funnel cake and dust with confectioners' sugar; drizzle with vanilla, chocolate, or caramel syrup; or top with cooked fruit, chocolate chip, candy pieces—whatever strikes your fancy!

Red Velvet Funnel Cakes

Crossroads Funnel Cakes, Rivertown Junction

A favorite layer cake turned into a delectable crispy fried indulgence! Just down the street from the replica of Dolly's Locust Ridge childhood home, the cooks at Crossroads swirl bright red batter into vats of sizzling oil, transforming it into one of Dollywood's most popular funnel cake flavors. Dusted with confectioners' sugar and finished with a rich cream cheese drizzle, this award-winning treat is surprisingly easy to create.

SERVES 2

For Cream Cheese Drizzle

2 ounces cream cheese (¼ block), softened
2 tablespoons unsalted butter, softened
½ teaspoon pure vanilla extract
½ cup confectioners' sugar
2 tablespoons whole milk

For Funnel Cakes

¾ cup buttermilk
1 large egg
1 cup all-purpose flour
½ teaspoon baking powder
1 tablespoon granulated sugar
¼ teaspoon salt
1 tablespoon unsweetened cocoa powder
¾ teaspoon white vinegar
5 drops red food coloring
1 quart canola oil
2 tablespoons confectioners' sugar

1. **To make Cream Cheese Drizzle:** Add cream cheese, butter, and vanilla to a medium bowl. Using a hand mixer, mix on medium-low speed until smooth.
2. Add confectioners' sugar and mix on low speed until combined. Add milk a tablespoon at a time, mixing after each addition, until glaze is thin enough to be drizzled. Add a little extra milk if needed. Set aside.
3. **To make Funnel Cakes:** In a small bowl, whisk together buttermilk and egg. In a medium bowl, stir together flour, baking powder, granulated sugar, salt, and cocoa powder.
4. Add wet ingredients to dry ingredients and mix well, making sure batter is smooth and without lumps.
5. Stir in vinegar, then add food coloring a few drops at a time, stirring after each addition, until batter is bright red.
6. In a wide sauté pan fitted with a thermometer, add oil 1½" deep and set over medium heat. Heat oil to 375°F.
7. Fill a squeeze bottle or funnel (with a ½" opening) with batter. Drizzle batter into hot oil in a swirling motion, beginning in the center and working your way out. Keep your motion smooth to avoid breaking the stream apart.

8. Fry batter 2 minutes or until darkened slightly. Use a pair of tongs to flip Funnel Cake over carefully. Fry an additional 45 seconds or until golden.

9. Transfer Funnel Cake to a large plate lined with paper towels and drain 1 minute. Dust with half of confectioners' sugar, and top with half of Cream Cheese Drizzle. Repeat with remaining batter. Serve.

Cooking Tip

Don't have a funnel or squeeze bottle? Spoon batter into a gallon-sized zip-top bag and use scissors to cut a ½" opening in one corner.

Kettle Korn

Country Cookers, Rivertown Junction

It's not only the salty-sweet aroma that will grab your attention as you approach the open-air displays at Country Cookers; it's also the sound! Dollywood hosts wearing thick gloves and face shields use long wooden paddles to stir the giant kettles of aggressively popping kernels, giving visitors an up-close view of how this iconic and delicious theme park snack is made. The original flavor used in this recipe is always available at the park, and there are also fun colors and flavors—think salted caramel and cherry cordial—that rotate throughout the season.

MAKES 8 CUPS

½ teaspoon popcorn salt
5 teaspoons granulated sugar
1 teaspoon packed light brown sugar
2 tablespoons canola oil
¼ cup popcorn kernels

1. Place a large baking sheet next to the stove. In a small bowl, stir together salt and both sugars.
2. In a 4-quart heavy-bottomed pot over medium-high heat, add oil and four kernels of popcorn. Place lid on pot.
3. Listen closely, and when you hear all four kernels pop, lift lid and add remaining kernels. Shake sugar mixture over the kernels evenly. Replace lid and shake pot for 5 seconds.
4. Continue shaking pot frequently as kernels begin to pop. As popping increases in speed, shake pot continuously.
5. When popping slows to 1–2 seconds between pops, immediately remove from heat and pour popcorn onto baking sheet.
6. Let cool 3 minutes and remove any unpopped kernels and burned pieces before serving.

Butterfly Pretzels

Mr. Jerry's Sit-N-Sip Refreshments, Craftsman's Valley

There's nothing quite like the experience of biting into a hot, soft pretzel with its golden, chewy crust, tender center, and crunchy salt. This is what theme park snack dreams are made of, and Dollywood does it up right with their adorable pretzels shaped like the park's universal symbol, the butterfly! They're available at multiple locations throughout the main park and in Splash Country; you can't throw a lasso without hitting one. Get creative with your homemade pretzels by varying the shape of your butterflies or trying other Dollywood-inspired shapes like hearts, water wheels, or bald eagles!

MAKES 8 PRETZELS

1 (¼-ounce) packet active dry yeast
4 teaspoons granulated sugar
1¼ cups warm water (110°F)
4 cups bread flour, divided
1 teaspoon table salt
3 teaspoons canola oil
⅓ cup baking soda
4 cups hot water
3 tablespoons coarse kosher salt

1. In a small bowl, sprinkle yeast and sugar over warm water and let sit 8 minutes or until mixture looks foamy.
2. In the bowl of a stand mixer fitted with paddle attachment, add 3 cups flour and table salt. Mix on low speed to combine. Add yeast mixture and oil and mix on low speed until a sticky dough is formed. Add flour 2 tablespoons at a time while mixing on low until a smooth dough is formed. You may not use all of the remaining 1 cup of flour.
3. Turn dough out onto lightly floured surface (or use dough hook attachment of stand mixer) and knead 8 minutes. Poke dough with your finger to create a deep dimple. If dimple fills back in quickly, you have kneaded long enough. If not, keep kneading and repeat poke test after another 2 minutes.
4. Place dough in a large lightly oiled bowl, turn to coat, cover with plastic wrap, and let rise in a warm place until doubled in size, about 1 hour.
5. Turn dough out onto a lightly floured surface, punch down gently, and divide into eight equal pieces. Roll each piece into a rope about 19" long.

continued on next page

6. Take loose ends of one rope and bring together to form a heart shape, twisting ends together to secure them in place. Bend bottom point of heart up to meet twisted ends and secure by pinching dough together. You should have what looks like a butterfly body with two wings. Bend center of each wing in to meet body, pinching dough to secure, and shape wing sections as desired. Bend center of bottom wing sections in to meet body, resulting in three sections on each wing. Repeat with remaining dough ropes. Let rest during next steps.
7. Alternate method: Instead of creating ropes, roll or pat out dough to ¾" thickness. Use a 4" butterfly cookie cutter to cut out shapes, then use a sharp knife to cut holes into the butterfly wing sections. You can use excess dough to make other shapes or pretzel bites to avoid waste. Let dough rest during next steps.
8. Preheat oven to 450°F and line two large baking sheets with parchment paper.
9. In a wide sauté pan over medium-high heat, dissolve baking soda in hot water. Bring to a boil, then reduce to a simmer over medium-low heat.
10. Use a wide slotted spatula sprayed with nonstick cooking spray to lower each butterfly into simmering water 8 seconds, then transfer to prepared sheets. Sprinkle immediately with kosher salt and bake 8 minutes or until deep golden brown.

Serving Tip

Go sweet or savory with dipping sauces. Stick with the classics like mustard or melted cheese sauce, or try a salty-sweet combo with hazelnut-chocolate spread, caramel, or cake frosting.

Homemade Pork Rinds

Pork Rinds, Craftsman's Valley

Craftsman's Valley is the place to shop for handmade gifts and souvenirs while watching master craftspeople demonstrate the creation process right in front of your eyes. It's no surprise, then, that you can also watch one of Dollywood's most famous snacks being made here: pork rinds! Transport your kitchen to the beautiful Smoky Mountains by making your own deliciously crispy Homemade Pork Rinds. This recipe is for barbecue-flavored pork rinds, but you can leave them plain—maybe sprinkled with a bit of salt—if you prefer.

SERVES 6

For Barbecue Seasoning

¼ cup paprika
3 tablespoons packed light brown sugar
2 teaspoons chili powder
1 teaspoon garlic powder
1½ teaspoons onion powder
1½ teaspoons ground black pepper
1½ teaspoons salt

For Pork Rinds

3 pounds pork back fat with skin, sliced into 2"-wide strips, fat removed from skin
1 quart canola oil

1. **To make Barbecue Seasoning:** Stir all ingredients together in a medium bowl and set aside.
2. **To make Pork Rinds:** Preheat oven to 250°F. Line a large baking sheet with parchment paper.
3. Cut pork strips into 1" sections and place on prepared sheet. Bake 3 hours or until skins are brown and dry to the touch.
4. In a wide sauté pan fitted with a thermometer, add oil 2" deep and set over medium heat. Heat oil to 375°F.
5. Working in batches, add dried pork skins to hot oil and fry 3 minutes or just until puffed and crispy. Use a slotted spatula to transfer to a large plate lined with paper towels.
6. Sprinkle with Barbecue Seasoning while still hot. Serve immediately.

Maple Popcorn Chicken

Sweets and Treats, Wildwood Grove

This Maple Popcorn Chicken is irresistible and unique thanks to the infusion of maple flavor into the breading. The original is served at Sweets and Treats, a walk-up snack stand nestled in Dollywood's Wildwood Grove expansion. This recipe can be fried or cooked in the oven.

SERVES 6

2 cups cold water
¼ cup plus 3 tablespoons pure maple syrup, divided
3 tablespoons kosher salt
3 (8-ounce) boneless, skinless chicken breasts
2 cups all-purpose flour
¼ teaspoon ground cinnamon
⅛ teaspoon ground nutmeg
2 teaspoons sea salt
1 teaspoon ground black pepper
2 large eggs
1 quart canola oil (for fry method)

1. In a medium bowl, stir together water, ¼ cup maple syrup, and kosher salt. Add chicken—use extra water if not fully covered—and refrigerate 1 hour.
2. In a second medium bowl, mix flour, cinnamon, nutmeg, sea salt, and pepper. In a third medium bowl, whisk eggs with remaining 3 tablespoons maple syrup.
3. Remove chicken from marinade, pat dry, and cut into 1" cubes.
4. Dip chicken cubes into flour mixture and gently shake off excess. Dip into egg and maple syrup mixture, letting drips fall back into container. Dip a final time into flour mixture, gently shake off excess, and place onto a clean work surface.
5. **Fry Method:** In a wide sauté pan fitted with a thermometer, add oil 2" deep and set over medium heat. Heat oil to 350°F. Working in batches, lower chicken cubes into hot oil and fry for about 4 minutes or until golden, crispy, and no longer pink in the centers. Use a slotted spoon to transfer to a large plate lined with paper towels.
6. **Oven Method:** Preheat oven to 400°F. Place an oven-safe metal rack onto a large baking sheet and spray generously with cooking spray. Place chicken cubes onto rack, leaving space between each one. Spray flour coating lightly with cooking spray. Bake 20 minutes or until centers are no longer pink.

Fried Cheese Curds

Jukebox Junction Food Truck, Dollywood's Splash Country

It's time for mozzarella sticks to take a seat, because these Fried Cheese Curds—with their mild, slightly salty molten centers and crispy golden breading—totally steal the show. Cheese curds are thought to have originated in ancient Rome with a dish called globuli: cheese curds coated with semolina flour, fried in olive oil, and rolled in honey. In Splash Country, you can grab a basket at the Jukebox Junction Food Truck after taking a dip in the pools. The breading gets some extra verve from a bit of beer added to the batter. You'll want to serve these fresh and hot, but take it slow and don't burn your mouth!

SERVES 8

1 pound cheese curds
2 tablespoons plus 1 cup all-purpose flour, divided
1½ teaspoons baking powder
½ teaspoon salt
½ teaspoon ground black pepper
¼ teaspoon garlic powder
2 large eggs, lightly beaten
½ cup buttermilk
½ cup beer (lager)
1 quart canola oil

1. Let curds sit in a large bowl at room temperature, about 20 minutes or until a sweat begins to form.
2. Toss curds with 2 tablespoons flour until lightly coated. Discard excess flour. Place curds on a large baking sheet and freeze 30 minutes.
3. In a medium bowl, add remaining 1 cup flour, baking powder, salt, pepper, and garlic powder. Stir to combine. Add eggs, buttermilk, and beer, and stir until batter is smooth.
4. In a large pot fitted with a thermometer, add oil 1½" deep and set over medium heat. Heat oil to 375°F.
5. Add cheese curds to batter and stir gently to make sure they are fully coated. Use a large, slotted spoon to remove curds and shake gently to let excess batter drip back into bowl.
6. Fry curds in oil 2 minutes or until golden and crispy. Work in batches to avoid crowding. Use a metal slotted spoon to transfer to a large plate lined with paper towels.

Dip it!

Fried Cheese Curds are delicious all by themselves, but you can try dipping them into any of your favorite sauces, like ketchup, honey mustard, ranch, tartar sauce, or brown gravy.

BeaverTails

BeaverTails, Dollywood's Splash Country

These wheat-dough pastries are stretched by hand to resemble the flat, oval shape of a beaver's tail, deep-fried, and finished with deliciously sweet toppings.

MAKES 12 BEAVERTAILS

For BeaverTails

½ cup warm water (110°F)
3 tablespoons plus ½ teaspoon granulated sugar, divided
1 (¼ ounce) packet active dry yeast
½ cup 2% warm milk (110°F)
¾ teaspoon salt
½ teaspoon pure vanilla extract
1 large egg, lightly beaten
3 tablespoons unsalted butter, melted
2½ cups whole-wheat flour
1 quart canola oil (for fry method)
4 tablespoons butter, melted (for oven method)

For Topping

½ cup granulated sugar
2 tablespoons ground cinnamon

1. **To make BeaverTails:** In the bowl of a stand mixer, add water and ½ teaspoon sugar. Sprinkle on yeast and let sit 5 minutes or until foamy.
2. Add remaining 3 tablespoons sugar, milk, salt, vanilla, egg, and butter to yeast mixture. Mix until combined. Add flour ½ cup at a time, mixing until just combined after each addition. Stop adding flour when a smooth dough forms—it should be slightly sticky but not wet. You might not use all of the flour.
3. Turn dough out onto a lightly floured surface (or use dough hook attachment of stand mixer) and knead until dough is smooth and elastic, about 8 minutes.
4. Place dough into a large lightly oiled bowl, turn to coat, and cover with plastic wrap. Let rise in a warm area 1 hour.
5. **To make Topping:** While dough is rising, stir together sugar with cinnamon in a small bowl. Set aside.
6. **To Assemble:** Punch down dough, cut into twelve equal pieces, and form into balls. Use your hands to stretch and shape each ball into ovals 6" long.
7. **Fry Method:** In a large pot fitted with a thermometer, add oil 2" deep and set over medium heat. Heat oil to 350°F. Fry each oval 1 minute on each side or until golden brown. Transfer to a baking sheet lined with paper towels, drain 10 seconds, and sprinkle generously with cinnamon sugar.

continued on next page

8. **Oven Method:** Preheat oven to 350°F. Line a large baking sheet with parchment paper and add the ovals side by side. Bake 20 minutes or until golden. Brush with butter and sprinkle with cinnamon sugar.

Serving Tip

Top your BeaverTails with pretty much anything you want! Try a squeeze of lemon with the classic cinnamon sugar version, chocolate-hazelnut spread with chopped banana, or peanut butter with chocolate drizzle. Add some crunch with chocolate chips or chopped nuts, or go fruity with a smear of fresh jam. You could even try a s'mores version using marshmallow crème, crumbled graham crackers, and chocolate syrup.

Plantain Chips with Mango Salsa (photo on next page)

Seasonal Culinary Booth, Dollywood's Flower & Food Festival

Plantains are the starchier, less-sweet cousins of bananas, and they are fabulous when sliced and baked or fried until perfectly crisp. Dip them into a bright Mango Salsa, and you've got one refreshing snack. Serve alone or as a side dish. A popular side served during Dollywood's celebration of springtime in the Smoky Mountains, this version is simple to create in your own kitchen.

SERVES 6

For Mango Salsa

2 large ripe mangoes, peeled, pitted, and small-diced
1 small red onion, peeled and small-diced
1 tablespoon minced pickled jalapeño peppers
½ cup finely chopped fresh cilantro
4 large Roma tomatoes, diced
¼ cup lime juice
⅛ teaspoon salt

For Plantain Chips

1 quart canola oil for frying or 3 tablespoons for baking
3 large green plantains, peeled, halved crosswise, and sliced lengthwise into thin slices
1½ teaspoons salt

1. **To make Mango Salsa:** In a large bowl, combine mangoes, onion, jalapeños, cilantro, and tomatoes. Drizzle in lime juice and toss to coat.
2. Season salsa with salt and stir. Cover bowl with plastic wrap and refrigerate 30 minutes.
3. **To make Plantain Chips (Fry Method):** Set a large sauté pan over medium heat and fit with a thermometer. Add oil 1½" deep and heat to 350°F. Working in batches, fry plantain slices—being careful not to crowd them—2 minutes. Flip them over and fry until golden, 2 or 3 minutes. Use tongs or a metal slotted spoon to transfer to a large plate lined with paper towels. Season with salt immediately.
4. **To make Plantain Chips (Oven Method):** Preheat oven to 350°F. Set two metal oven-safe racks over two large baking sheets. Arrange plantain slices on rack, being careful not to overlap. Brush with oil, flip slices over, and brush other side with oil. Season with salt. Bake 20 minutes or until golden and crispy, rotating sheets halfway through.

Sweet Potato Poutine

Market Square BIG SKILLET®, Rivertown Junction, Harvest Festival

Poutine is a ubiquitous Canadian dish that consists of French fries topped with brown gravy and fresh cheese curds. During Dollywood's Harvest Festival, you can try a unique twist on the tasty combination. This version starts with a pile of hot waffle-cut sweet potato fries topped with salty applewood-smoked bacon, crispy fried onions, and sliced green onions. The combo is drizzled with a luxurious homemade white Cheddar sauce that comes together quickly and easily. Take a bite, and be transported to a crisp and colorful fall in the Smoky Mountains.

SERVES 2

2 tablespoons unsalted butter
2 tablespoons all-purpose flour
1 cup whole milk
½ teaspoon salt
1 cup shredded sharp white Cheddar cheese
4 cups frozen waffle-cut sweet potato fries
4 slices applewood-smoked bacon, cooked crisp and crumbled
¼ cup French-fried onions
¼ cup sliced green onions

1. In a small saucepan over medium-low heat, melt butter. Sprinkle in flour and whisk to form a paste.
2. Add milk and salt to pan, then cook 5 minutes or until mixture starts to thicken, whisking constantly to remove all lumps. Add cheese and stir 5 minutes or until melted and remove from heat. Drizzle in a little extra milk to thin sauce if needed.
3. Cook sweet potato fries according to instructions on package. Divide among two plates and top with crumbled bacon, French-fried onions, and green onions. Drizzle with cheese sauce.

Sweet Corn Hushpuppies

Market Square BIG SKILLET®, Rivertown Junction, Harvest Festival

During the fall Harvest Festival, you can pick up these sweet and crunchy corn hushpuppies in the park. What do hushpuppies have to do with fall, you may ask? This snack gets drizzled with a kicked-up aioli that has a secret and autumn-appropriate ingredient: pumpkin! Stick to a modest drizzle for a flavor accent, or double the aioli ingredients for some deep-dipping action.

MAKES 18 HUSHPUPPIES

For Pumpkin Sriracha Aioli

3 medium cloves roasted garlic, peeled and minced
¼ cup pumpkin purée
¼ cup mayonnaise
2 tablespoons sriracha
1 teaspoon lemon juice
⅛ teaspoon salt

For Sweet Corn Hushpuppies

1½ cups finely ground yellow cornmeal
½ cup self-rising flour
1½ teaspoons baking powder
½ teaspoon baking soda
¾ teaspoon salt
1 tablespoon granulated sugar
½ cup canned sweet corn kernels, drained
1 large egg, lightly beaten
¾ cup buttermilk, divided
1 quart canola oil
½ cup chopped scallions

1. **To make Pumpkin Sriracha Aioli:** In a medium bowl, whisk together garlic, pumpkin purée, mayonnaise, sriracha, lemon juice, and salt. Refrigerate until ready to use.
2. **To make Sweet Corn Hushpuppies:** In a large bowl, combine cornmeal, flour, baking powder, baking soda, salt, sugar, and corn kernels. Add egg and ¼ cup buttermilk. Stir to form a thick batter. Drizzle in remaining ½ cup buttermilk while stirring. Stop adding buttermilk when batter resembles cookie dough. You may not use all of the buttermilk. Let batter rest at least 10 minutes while completing next step.
3. In a large sauté pan fitted with a thermometer, add oil 2½" deep and set over medium heat. Heat oil to 350°F.
4. Working in batches, drop heaping tablespoons of batter into hot oil and fry 3 minutes or just until hushpuppies are deep golden. Transfer to a large plate lined with paper towels.
5. Serve hushpuppies warm, drizzled with aioli and topped with scallions.

Hazelnut Churros

Sweets and Treats, Wildwood Grove, Dollywood's Smoky Mountain Christmas

Classic cinnamon sugar churros can always be found in the fantastical land of Wildwood Grove, but it's only during the Smoky Mountain Christmas festival that you can try this fun variation loaded with hazelnuts and served with chocolate-hazelnut spread for dipping. Dollywood fans describe this as a holiday treat that's not to be missed. And now you don't have to wait until festival time in the park: You'll have a blast re-creating this version at any time of the year.

MAKES 16 CHURROS

- ½ heaping cup whole hazelnuts
- 8 tablespoons (1 stick) unsalted butter, divided
- ½ cup plus 2 tablespoons granulated sugar, divided
- 1 cup water
- 1 teaspoon pure vanilla extract
- 1 cup plus 2 tablespoons all-purpose flour
- ½ teaspoon salt
- 2 large eggs
- 1 tablespoon ground cinnamon
- 1 quart canola oil (for fry method)
- ½ cup chocolate-hazelnut spread, warmed

1. Place hazelnuts in a food processor and pulse until a fine consistency is reached. Do not overprocess, or oils will be released and the texture will start to resemble butter.
2. In a medium saucepan over medium heat, add 6 tablespoons butter, 2 tablespoons sugar, and water. Bring to a boil, then remove from heat.
3. Use a nonstick spatula to stir vanilla, flour, salt, and ¼ cup powdered hazelnuts into pan. Continue stirring and scraping down bowl until mixture is thickened, about 1 minute. Let cool 15 minutes.
4. Using a hand mixer, add eggs to cooled dough one at a time, mixing after each addition, until combined. Chill dough in refrigerator 20 minutes.
5. Line a large rimmed baking sheet with parchment paper. Transfer dough to a large piping bag fitted with a large (½") closed star tip. Pipe 6"-lengths of dough onto prepared sheet and freeze 30 minutes.
6. While churros are in freezer, stir together remaining powdered hazelnuts, remaining ½ cup sugar, and cinnamon in a shallow container with a flat bottom.

continued on next page

7. **Fry Method:** In a wide sauté pan fitted with a thermometer, add oil 1½" deep and set over medium heat. Heat oil to 375°F. Working in batches, fry churros 4 minutes or until deep golden, turning halfway through. Don't crowd pan, or churros will stick together. Transfer to a large plate lined with paper towels, drain 10 seconds, then roll in cinnamon-hazelnut sugar.
8. **Oven Method:** Preheat oven to 350°F. Remove baking sheet from freezer and bake on center rack 20 minutes, then turn oven to broil on high and broil until golden, checking every 2 minutes. Melt remaining 2 tablespoons butter in a small bowl, brush onto churros, and roll churros in cinnamon-hazelnut sugar.
9. Serve churros with warm chocolate-hazelnut spread on the side for dipping.

Change It Up

Use a smaller or larger pastry tip to vary the size of your churros. Smaller tips will yield narrow "churro fries," while larger tips will create the thick churros available in the park. Keep in mind that bake or fry times will change depending on the thickness of the churro, so watch them closely until golden on the outside and cooked through.

CHAPTER FOUR

Lunch in the Foothills

Have some midday hunger? This chapter has got you covered. These recipes are a collection of powerhouse lunchtime favorites consisting of all kinds of amazing sandwiches, pizza, nachos, and more, all inspired by quick walk-up meal options in Dollywood and Dollywood's Splash Country. And yes, you'll even learn to make those big ol' juicy turkey legs from the park—the perfect grab-and-go lunch! Scale up these recipes to feed a crowd or choose several to create a Dollywood-themed buffet that would make Dolly herself give a well-manicured thumbs-up. Pair any of these items with a tall glass of Sweet Tea from Chapter 9 and take an afternoon siesta on the porch (rocking chair recommended).

Cheesesteak Sandwiches

Market Square BIG SKILLET®, Rivertown Junction

The mouthwatering aroma of sizzling steak, sausage, peppers, and onions on the giant skillets in the Market Square pavilion is hard to miss. The tantalizing options on the BIG SKILLET® menu change all the time, but this sandwich—Dollywood's own twist on a Philly cheesesteak sandwich—is a constant staple and fan favorite. When re-creating this iconic dish, be patient with cooking down the vegetables until very tender. Top with as little or as much of the savory cheese sauce as you want, and enjoy this exciting and satisfying lunchtime meal.

SERVES 4

- 1½ pounds flank steak
- 2 teaspoons salt
- 1 teaspoon ground black pepper
- ¾ teaspoon dry mustard
- 2 tablespoons olive oil
- 1 large red bell pepper, seeded, cored, and sliced thin
- 1 large orange bell pepper, seeded, cored, and sliced thin
- 1 large green bell pepper, seeded, cored, and sliced thin
- 1 large yellow onion, peeled and sliced thin
- 4 hoagie buns
- 1 recipe white Cheddar sauce from Sweet Potato Poutine (see recipe in Chapter 3)

1. Rub both sides of steak with salt, black pepper, and dry mustard. Slice diagonally against the grain, keeping slices very thin. Set aside.
2. Heat oil in a large skillet over medium-high heat. Add bell peppers and onion. Sauté until very soft and aromatic, about 15 minutes. Remove to a large plate. If skillet looks dry, drizzle in a little more oil.
3. Add sliced steak to skillet and cook to desired level of doneness, tossing frequently. Cook time will vary depending on thickness of slices—check every 3 minutes.
4. Add cooked peppers and onions back to skillet with steak, stir, and remove from heat. Serve in hoagie buns topped with white Cheddar sauce.

Change It Up

If you want to make the Sausage and Potato Big Skillet on Market Square's menu, substitute 14 ounces sliced smoked sausage for the steak and add 1 pound thinly sliced red potatoes. Sauté potatoes in olive oil for 10 minutes before adding the peppers and onions. Season with salt, pepper, and chopped parsley; sauté until tender; then add smoked sausage until warmed through. Yum!

Footlong Corn Dogs

Dogs N Taters, Rivertown Junction

Is there a more convenient theme park lunch than a corn dog? It is portable, comes on a stick, and is perfect for munching while exploring Rivertown Junction—or just lounging around the house. The next time you are at the park, grab one before wandering over to the water to enjoy the fountains while keeping an eye out for ducks and turtles. Just like the park, this recipe uses footlong hot dogs, and the deep-fried batter has a delicious cornmeal crunch with a tiny hint of sweetness. Oh, and don't worry if you can't find footlong hot dogs; regular size works (just make double the amount!).

SERVES 6

1 cup all-purpose flour
1 cup yellow cornmeal
¼ teaspoon ground black pepper
¾ teaspoon salt
4 teaspoons baking powder
3 tablespoons amber honey
1 large egg, lightly beaten
1 cup whole milk
¼ cup cornstarch
1 quart canola oil
6 footlong hot dogs

1. In a long container with a flat bottom, stir together flour, cornmeal, pepper, salt, and baking powder. Mix in honey, egg, and milk until a smooth batter forms. Refrigerate 45 minutes.
2. Insert a long wooden skewer ⅔ of the way into each hot dog and pat hot dogs dry with a paper towel. Rub a small amount of cornstarch onto each hot dog. Shake off excess.
3. In a wide sauté pan fitted with a thermometer, add oil 2½" deep and set over medium heat. Heat to 365°F.
4. Dip hot dogs in cold batter and roll, making sure there's a thick layer of batter on all sides. Working in batches, lower hot dogs into oil, fry 10 seconds, then flip over. Continue frying 2½ minutes more or until deep golden, turning once halfway through. Use tongs to transfer to a large plate lined with paper towels to drain 2 minutes before serving.

Serving Tip

For the real park experience, serve these corn dogs with the Tater Twirls from Chapter 6 and don't forget to add your favorite condiments like ketchup and mustard.

Frannie's Famous Fried Chicken Sandwiches

Grandstand Café, Country Fair

Seasoned Dollywood lovers will tell you that if you have to pick just one lunch item in the park, go for this blue ribbon award–winning fried chicken sandwich! This noteworthy sandwich contains chicken breast that is marinated in pickle juice. When making this sandwich at home, finish it off with your favorite condiments, such as mayonnaise, ketchup, mustard, Thousand Island dressing, or barbecue sauce! Enjoy with a side of fries for the full park experience.

SERVES 2

2 (4-ounce) boneless, skinless chicken breasts
½ cup buttermilk
1 cup dill pickle juice, divided
¼ cup cornstarch
2 large eggs
½ cup all-purpose flour
¾ teaspoon salt
½ teaspoon ground black pepper
2 teaspoons confectioners' sugar
1 quart canola oil (for fry method)
2 large hamburger buns, toasted
2 large slices ripe globe tomato
4 medium leaves green leaf lettuce

1. Place chicken between two pieces of plastic wrap. Use flat side of a meat tenderizer to pound until breasts are of even thickness.
2. In a gallon-sized zip-top bag, add buttermilk and ⅔ cup pickle juice. Place chicken breasts in liquid so they are fully submerged. Seal bag and refrigerate 2 hours.
3. In a shallow, flat-bottomed container, add cornstarch. In a second shallow, flat-bottomed container, whisk eggs with remaining ⅓ cup pickle juice. In a third shallow, flat-bottomed container, stir together flour, salt, pepper, and sugar.
4. Remove chicken from marinade and let excess drip back into bag. Dredge in cornstarch, coating both sides, and shake off excess. Dip chicken into egg mixture, letting excess drip back into container. Dredge chicken in flour mixture, making sure both sides are fully coated, and set onto a clean work surface.
5. **Fry Method:** In a wide sauté pan fitted with a thermometer over medium heat, add oil 1½" deep. Heat to 375°F. Fry chicken 4 minutes on each side or until golden brown and cooked to an internal temperature of 165°F. Use tongs to transfer to a large plate lined with paper towels.

continued on next page

6. **Oven Method:** Preheat oven to 400°F. Place a metal oven-safe rack over a medium baking sheet and spray generously with cooking spray. Place chicken on rack, leaving room between each piece, and spray flour coating lightly with cooking spray. Bake 30 minutes, flipping halfway through or until golden and cooked to an internal temperature of 165°F.
7. Serve chicken on toasted buns topped with tomato and lettuce.

Turkey Legs

Miss Lillian's BBQ Corner, Craftsman's Valley

If you've visited Dollywood before, you have probably seen park visitors wandering the paths of the park gnawing on massive turkey legs that are certainly larger than anything you've seen on your Thanksgiving table. Why so big? Theme parks and Renaissance fairs typically use legs from tom turkeys that weigh up to 50 pounds each! Huge turkey = huge legs. Dollywood smokes their delicious turkey legs, but this recipe has been transformed so you can make your own theme park turkey legs using your oven. Add a couple of your favorite side dishes from Chapter 6 and call it a meal.

SERVES 3

- 4 cups water
- 2 tablespoons liquid smoke
- 3 tablespoons packed light brown sugar
- 3 tablespoons salt
- 1¾ teaspoons ground black pepper, divided
- 3 (16-ounce) tom turkey legs with skin
- 3 tablespoons salted butter, melted
- 2 teaspoons chili powder
- ¾ teaspoon smoked paprika
- ¾ teaspoon onion powder

1. In a large bowl, add water, liquid smoke, brown sugar, salt, and 1 teaspoon pepper. Stir, and add turkey legs. Add extra water if legs are not fully submerged. Refrigerate 4 hours or overnight.
2. Preheat oven to 400°F. Line a large rimmed baking sheet with aluminum foil.
3. Remove turkey legs from brine and pat dry. In a small bowl, stir together melted butter, chili powder, paprika, onion powder, and remaining ¾ teaspoon pepper. Brush onto turkey legs and place skin side down on prepared sheet.
4. Roast on center rack 25 minutes, then reduce heat to 325°F and continue roasting an additional 40 minutes or until the internal temperature of the turkey is 165°F.
5. Let turkey legs rest 20 minutes before serving.

BBQ Pork Sandwiches

Hickory House BBQ, Craftsman's Valley

Amusement Business magazine declared Dollywood's BBQ Pork Sandwich to be the best pork barbecue of any theme park in the country—quite an endorsement! While the pork at Dollywood is smoked on site, not everyone has a smoker sitting around at home. This simplified slow cooker version has the same flavor profile used in the park and results in a mountain of fall-apart-tender pulled pork that is finger-lickin' good.

SERVES 8

4 medium cloves garlic, peeled and minced
2 teaspoons onion powder
1 teaspoon ground black pepper
1 tablespoon seasoned salt
1 teaspoon ground cumin
1 teaspoon celery salt
1½ teaspoons smoked paprika
1½ teaspoons dry mustard
¼ cup packed light brown sugar
1 (6-pound) pork shoulder
1¼ teaspoons liquid smoke
1 cup water
2 teaspoons apple cider vinegar
1 tablespoon Worcestershire sauce
8 hamburger buns
1 cup smoky barbecue sauce

1. In a small bowl, stir together garlic, onion powder, pepper, seasoned salt, cumin, celery salt, paprika, dry mustard, and brown sugar. Rub seasoning onto pork shoulder. Place pork in a large bowl and refrigerate overnight.
2. In a small bowl, stir together liquid smoke, water, vinegar, and Worcestershire. Place pork and any excess dry rub from bowl in a large slow cooker fat side up. Pour liquid mixture around bottom of pork. Cover, and cook on low 8–10 hours until pork is extremely tender and falls apart when pierced with a fork.
3. Transfer pork to a cutting board and use two large forks to shred meat, discarding bone, cartilage, and large pieces of fat. Pour liquid from slow cooker into a large heat-resistant bowl. Return pork to slow cooker and top with ¾ cup liquid. Stir, and drizzle in extra liquid as needed until pork is moistened. Discard unused liquid.
4. Serve pork on hamburger buns topped with a drizzle of barbecue sauce.

Smoke It

If you do have a smoker, plan on smoking at 250°F for about 1 hour and 15 minutes per pound. Rub pork with dry seasoning before placing in the smoker, and smoke until internal temperature of pork is 165°F. Baste with wet seasoning (omit liquid smoke), wrap with aluminum foil, and continue smoking until internal temperature is between 190°F and 205°F and meat is extremely tender.

Smoky Mountain Nachos

Till & Harvest, Wildwood Grove

Till & Harvest offers a pleasing assortment of Mexican-inspired dishes. The menu is arranged in a build-your-own style where you can pick from combinations of ingredients to create a burrito, bowl, or salad. These nachos are a popular menu item, and with a mountain of tasty tidbits like queso drizzle and avocado crema, what's not to love?

SERVES 4

- 1 cup plus 2 tablespoons half-and-half, divided
- 1 pound white American cheese, grated
- ¼ teaspoon chili powder
- ¾ teaspoon salt, divided
- ¼ teaspoon ground black pepper
- 2 medium-sized ripe avocados, peeled, pitted, and sliced
- ½ cup sour cream
- 2 tablespoons lime juice
- ¼ teaspoon garlic powder
- 6 cups tortilla chips
- ½ pulled pork recipe from BBQ Pork Sandwiches (see recipe in this chapter)
- 1 (12-ounce) container pico de gallo
- 1 large ripe globe tomato, diced
- 1 small red onion, peeled and diced
- 1½ cups shredded iceberg lettuce
- ⅓ cup pickled jalapeño slices

1. In a medium heavy-bottomed pot over medium heat, add 1 cup half-and-half and cheese. Cook 6 minutes or until cheese melts, whisking constantly to prevent clumps. When queso is smooth, stir in chili powder, ½ teaspoon salt, and pepper. If queso is too thick, whisk in additional half-and-half 1 tablespoon at a time until desired consistency has been reached. Remove from heat.
2. In a blender, add avocado, sour cream, lime juice, garlic powder, and remaining ¼ teaspoon salt. Blend until smooth. Taste, and add more salt if needed.
3. Divide tortilla chips evenly among four plates. Top with pulled pork, queso, pico de gallo, tomato, onion, lettuce, jalapeño, and avocado crema.

Lumber Jack Pizza (photo on next spread)

Lumber Jack's Pizza, Timber Canyon

Though Lumber Jack's now specializes in personal-sized pizzas, they were once known for their massive 30" 12-pound showcase pie loaded with meaty toppings. For a time, they even had an eating challenge that awarded Super Gold season passes to any three people who could eat the whole giant pizza in 1 hour! This recipe replicates their meat lover's Lumber Jack Pizza.

SERVES 3

- 4¼ cups bread flour, divided
- 2 teaspoons salt, divided
- 1 teaspoon instant yeast
- 2½ teaspoons granulated sugar, divided
- 3 tablespoons olive oil
- 1⅓ cups warm water (110°F)
- 1 (8-ounce) can tomato sauce
- 3 tablespoons tomato paste
- 1 tablespoon Italian seasoning
- ¾ teaspoon garlic powder, divided
- ½ teaspoon onion powder
- ¼ teaspoon crushed red pepper flakes
- ¼ cup yellow cornmeal
- 8 ounces shredded mozzarella cheese
- 4 slices applewood-smoked bacon, cooked crisp and crumbled
- ⅔ cup cooked ground pork sausage
- 18 slices pepperoni
- 3 tablespoons salted butter, melted

1. In the bowl of a stand mixer fitted with a dough hook, add 4 cups flour, 1½ teaspoons salt, yeast, and 2 teaspoons sugar. Mix on low speed until combined. Add oil and water and mix on medium-low speed 2 minutes. If dough is wet and sticky, add remaining ¼ cup flour 1 tablespoon at a time until an elastic, stretchy dough is formed. You may not use all of the flour. Mix an additional 3 minutes.
2. Turn dough out onto lightly floured surface and separate into three equal pieces. Shape each piece into a ball and place in separate medium lightly oiled bowls. Cover bowls with plastic and let rise in a warm place until doubled in size, about 1 hour.
3. While dough is rising, prepare pizza sauce: In a small saucepan over medium-low heat, stir together tomato sauce, tomato paste, Italian seasoning, ½ teaspoon garlic powder, onion powder, red pepper flakes, remaining ½ teaspoon sugar, and remaining ½ teaspoon salt. Let simmer, stirring occasionally, 30 minutes. Remove from heat.
4. Place a large pizza stone in oven and preheat to 400°F. Sprinkle cornmeal onto center of two large rimless baking sheets. Note: If you don't have a pizza stone, bake pizzas directly on rimless baking sheets, but do not preheat them.

continued on next page

5. Punch down dough balls, turn out onto a lightly floured surface, and roll out into three 8" discs. Place discs onto cornmeal on baking sheets and top with pizza sauce, cheese, bacon, sausage, and pepperoni.
6. Use a large flat spatula to transfer pizzas to hot pizza stone. Bake 12 minutes or until crust edges are deep golden. Transfer pizzas back to baking sheet and turn off oven, leaving pizza stone inside to cool. If your stone is not big enough for all pizzas, bake them one or two at a time.
7. In a small bowl, stir together melted butter with remaining ¼ teaspoon garlic powder. Brush onto edges of pizza crust, slice, and serve.

Nashville Hot Chicken Sliders

Jukebox Junction Food Truck, Dollywood's Splash Country

After hanging ten in the Mountain Waves wave pool, grab a towel and look for the big blue truck with the shiny silver chicken-shaped hood ornament not far behind the loungers—that's where you'll find these Nashville Hot Chicken Sliders. The famous spicy heat in the chicken comes from a quadruple whammy of sources: a spicy-sweet marinade, a hot-sauce egg wash, a cayenne-spiced dredge, and a potent sauce to brush on the finished fowl.

MAKES 6 SLIDERS

- 2½ cups buttermilk, divided
- 5 teaspoons cayenne pepper, divided
- ¾ teaspoon garlic powder, divided
- 3 tablespoons packed dark brown sugar, divided
- 4 teaspoons ground black pepper, divided
- 1½ pounds boneless, skinless chicken thighs, cut to fit slider buns
- 4 teaspoons salt, divided
- ⅓ cup cornstarch
- 2 cups all-purpose flour
- 2½ teaspoons paprika, divided
- ¼ cup hot sauce
- 1 large egg
- 1 quart canola oil (for fry method)
- ½ cup olive oil
- ½ teaspoon chili powder
- 6 slider buns

1. To a gallon-sized zip-top bag, add 1½ cups buttermilk, 2 teaspoons cayenne pepper, ½ teaspoon garlic powder, 2 tablespoons brown sugar, and 1½ teaspoons black pepper. Gently shake bag to mix ingredients.
2. Add chicken to bag, making sure the pieces are covered by the liquid. Seal bag and refrigerate at least 2 hours or up to overnight.
3. Remove chicken from marinade and pat dry. Season both sides with 2 teaspoons salt and ½ teaspoon black pepper. Let sit on counter 20 minutes.
4. In a shallow container with a wide bottom, add cornstarch. In a second shallow container with a wide bottom, stir together flour, 2 teaspoons cayenne pepper, 2 teaspoons paprika, remaining 2 teaspoons salt, and remaining 2 teaspoons black pepper. In a third shallow container with a wide bottom, whisk remaining 1 cup buttermilk, hot sauce, and egg.
5. Dredge both sides of a piece of chicken in cornstarch and shake off excess. Dip chicken into buttermilk mixture, making sure it is fully submerged, and let excess drip off. Dredge both sides of chicken into flour mixture, making sure they are coated well. Set on a clean surface and repeat with remaining chicken pieces.

continued on next page

6. **Fry Method:** In a wide sauté pan fitted with a thermometer, add canola oil 1½" deep and set over medium heat. Heat to 375°F. Fry chicken 7 minutes per side or until golden brown and centers are cooked to an internal temperature of 170°F. Use tongs to transfer chicken to a large plate lined with paper towels.
7. **Oven Method:** Preheat oven to 400°F. Place a metal oven-safe rack over a large baking sheet and spray generously with cooking spray. Place chicken on rack, leaving room between each piece, and spray flour coating lightly with cooking spray. Bake 40 minutes, flipping chicken halfway through, or just until centers are cooked to an internal temperature of 170°F.
8. In a small bowl, whisk olive oil, remaining 1 teaspoon cayenne pepper, remaining 1 tablespoon brown sugar, remaining ½ teaspoon paprika, remaining ¼ teaspoon garlic powder, and chili powder. Brush sauce lightly over chicken. Serve chicken on slider buns.

Butterfly Wrap

The Cascades Concessions, Dollywood's Splash Country

While Dollywood and Splash Country have no lack of traditional Southern fare, deep-fried snacks, and rich desserts, there are plenty of lighter options available as well. This Butterfly Wrap—available at both Cascades Concessions and the Watering Hole—is a popular choice that is perfect whether you are lounging poolside or eating on the go. The tomato basil tortilla and homemade honey Dijon dressing add tons of zippy flavor to this easy lunch dish.

SERVES 1

2 tablespoons Dijon mustard
2 teaspoons amber honey
½ teaspoon olive oil
⅛ teaspoon ground ginger
⅛ teaspoon garlic salt
⅛ teaspoon ground black pepper
1 (10") tomato basil tortilla
2 large leaves romaine lettuce, trimmed
2 thin slices Cheddar cheese
2 thin slices (2 ounces) deli ham
2 thin slices (2 ounces) deli turkey
3 slices ripe globe tomato

1. In a small bowl, mix together mustard, honey, oil, ginger, garlic salt, and pepper. Spread onto tortilla.
2. Layer lettuce, cheese, ham, turkey, and tomato on tortilla. Make sure to leave space around the outside of tortilla.
3. Fold both ends of tortilla toward the center, then roll tightly from bottom to top.

Frito Pie

Dogs N Taters, Dollywood's Splash Country

The origin of Frito Pie is a story that has a fair bit of dispute. In New Mexico, the claim is that the dish started at a five-and-dime general store in Santa Fe in the 1960s, with the original having no toppings other than homemade chili scooped into opened bags of corn chips. In Texas, locals claim that the mother of the supposed inventor of Fritos—Daisy Dean Doolin—was the first one to concoct a Frito Pie—complete with cheese and onions—in the 1930s. However, company records show that the layered snack was first seen in a recipe booklet during a company campaign for the product. Whichever story you believe, this is a tasty combination that can be made directly in a bag of corn chips or layered in a bowl.

SERVES 4

2 teaspoons olive oil
1 small yellow onion, peeled and finely chopped
8 ounces ground chuck
2 medium cloves garlic, peeled and minced
1 (14-ounce) can fire-roasted crushed tomatoes, including juice
1 (14-ounce) can kidney beans, drained, unrinsed
3 tablespoons chili powder
½ teaspoon salt
½ teaspoon ground black pepper
6 cups Fritos corn chips
2 cups shredded sharp Cheddar cheese
1 cup diced fresh Roma tomato
¾ cup chopped scallions
½ cup sour cream

1. Heat oil in a medium pot over medium heat. Add onion and cook 3 minutes, stirring frequently. Add ground chuck and break into small pieces using a spatula. Cook, stirring frequently, 8 minutes or until beef is cooked through. Drain, leaving a small amount of grease in pot.
2. Add garlic, tomatoes, beans, chili powder, salt, and pepper to pot. Bring to a boil over high heat, then reduce heat to low. Cook uncovered, stirring occasionally, 25 minutes or until chili thickens.
3. Distribute corn chips among four bowls. Top with chili, cheese, tomato, scallions, and sour cream.

Beef Bulgogi Nachos (photo on next spread)

Seasonal Culinary Booth, Dollywood's Flower & Food Festival

Bulgogi—also known as Korean beef barbecue—is composed of very thin slices of beef marinated in a delightfully sweet combination of Korean flavors, then cooked and served, either on its own, over a bed of rice, or with lettuce leaves. During the springtime Flower & Food Festival, Dollywood elevates this widely loved Korean dish into something special: a big pile of wonton chip nachos topped with sriracha crema, sliced green onions, and alfalfa sprouts.

SERVES 4

For Beef Bulgogi

1½ pounds ribeye steak
½ cup grated Asian pear
2 tablespoons packed light brown sugar
2½ tablespoons toasted sesame oil, divided
¼ cup soy sauce
1 tablespoon gochujang paste
¼ cup minced yellow onion
4 medium cloves garlic, peeled and minced
¼ teaspoon ground ginger
½ teaspoon salt
1 cup sour cream
2 tablespoons sriracha
2 tablespoons lime juice
⅔ cup chopped scallions
1 cup alfalfa sprouts

For Wonton Chips

20 wonton wrappers
1 quart canola oil (for fry method)

1. **To make Beef Bulgogi:** Wrap steak in plastic and freeze 30 minutes. Remove plastic wrap and use a sharp knife to cut steak into ⅛" slices.
2. In a gallon-sized zip-top bag, add pear, brown sugar, 2 tablespoons sesame oil, soy sauce, gochujang, onion, garlic, ginger, and salt. Gently shake bag to mix ingredients. Add steak, seal bag, shake, and refrigerate 2 hours.
3. While steak is marinating, mix sour cream, sriracha, and lime juice in a small bowl. Cover and refrigerate until ready to serve.
4. Heat remaining ½ tablespoon sesame oil in a large skillet over medium-high heat. Remove beef from marinade and add to skillet in a single layer. Cook 2 minutes on each side or until beef reaches desired level of doneness. Remove from heat and wrap in aluminum foil to keep warm until ready to serve.
5. **To make Wonton Chips:** Use a pizza cutter to cut wonton wrappers diagonally from corner to corner, creating four triangles per wrapper.

continued on next page

6. **Fry Method:** In a wide sauté pan fitted with a thermometer, add canola oil 1½" deep and set over medium heat. Heat oil to 360°F. Working in batches, fry wrappers 2 minutes or until golden and crispy. Use a wide metal slotted spatula to transfer chips to a large plate lined with paper towels.
7. **Oven Method:** Preheat oven to 400°F. Line two large baking sheets with parchment paper. Arrange wrappers on sheets and brush both sides of triangles with a small amount of oil. Bake 15 minutes, turning every 5 minutes until chips are golden. Transfer to cooling rack.
8. Serve Wonton Chips layered with Beef Bulgogi, sriracha crema, scallions, and alfalfa sprouts.

Lobster Rolls

Seasonal Culinary Booth, Dollywood's Flower & Food Festival

The treats served at Dollywood's springtime festival will make your taste buds do a happy dance—especially this classic Maine lobster roll! For this version, use frozen cooked lobster meat to keep it easy and thaw according to package instructions. If you prefer fresh, use the meat from two or three large boiled lobsters instead. To mimic the festival's dish, serve these rolls with salt and vinegar potato chips.

SERVES 4

- 1 pound cooked lobster meat, rinsed and patted dry
- ¼ cup finely chopped celery
- ¼ cup mayonnaise
- 1 tablespoon lemon juice
- ½ teaspoon Old Bay seasoning
- ½ teaspoon salt
- ½ teaspoon ground black pepper
- 4 tablespoons unsalted butter, melted
- ½ teaspoon celery seed
- 4 New England (split-top) hot dog buns

1. In a large bowl, stir together lobster meat, celery, mayonnaise, lemon juice, Old Bay, salt, and pepper.
2. Heat a large skillet over medium heat. In a small bowl, mix melted butter with celery seed. Spread butter mixture onto outer sides of buns. Toast both sides of buns in skillet, about 2 minutes per side.
3. Divide lobster mixture evenly between buns and serve.

Did You Know?

Maine-style lobster rolls use cold lobster meat and a mayo-based dressing, while Connecticut-style rolls use warm lobster meat coated with butter.

Harvest Flatbread

Iron Horse Pizza, The Village, Harvest Festival

Fall at Dollywood is arguably the most exciting time for any foodie to visit the park. The Harvest Festival adds seasonal menu items to existing food establishments as well as temporary pop-up booths with even more delightful options. This flatbread is available at both Lumber Jack's Pizza in Timber Canyon and Iron Horse Pizza in The Village. It is so easy to re-create at home.

MAKES 2 FLATBREADS

2 tablespoons pure maple syrup
4 teaspoons olive oil, divided
1 teaspoon lemon juice
½ teaspoon salt, divided
½ teaspoon ground black pepper, divided
1 large sweet potato, peeled and cut into 1" cubes
3 tablespoons unsalted butter
1 large sweet onion, peeled and sliced
2 (7-ounce) prebaked flatbreads
8 pieces applewood-smoked bacon, cooked crisp and crumbled
½ cup shredded mozzarella cheese
½ cup shredded smoked Gouda

1. Preheat oven to 400°F. Line a large baking sheet with parchment paper.
2. In a small bowl, stir together maple syrup, 2 teaspoons oil, lemon juice, ¼ teaspoon salt, and ¼ teaspoon pepper. Add sweet potato cubes and toss until fully coated. Place on prepared sheet and roast 45 minutes, stirring and turning every 15 minutes or until potatoes are tender.
3. While potatoes are roasting, melt butter in a large skillet over medium heat. Add onion and stir to coat. Sauté 5 minutes or until onion starts to soften, stirring frequently. Reduce heat to low and cook uncovered, stirring occasionally, until onion is deeply golden and aromatic, about 40 minutes.
4. When potatoes are done, remove from oven and increase temperature to 425°F. Transfer roasted potatoes to a medium bowl and discard parchment paper. Place flatbreads directly on baking sheet and brush with remaining 2 teaspoons oil.
5. Top flatbreads with roasted potatoes, caramelized onion, bacon, mozzarella, and Gouda. Season with remaining ¼ teaspoon salt and remaining ¼ teaspoon pepper.
6. Bake flatbreads on center rack 6 minutes or until cheese has melted and flatbread is crispy on bottom. Slice and serve warm.

CHAPTER FIVE

Dinner with Dolly

Dolly Parton is vocal about her experiences growing up in the mountains of East Tennessee. In her childhood home, food was a love language that has left a lasting impression on her to this day. The story of Dolly's life is expressed throughout Dollywood not only visually and musically but also culinarily through robust menus filled with storied dishes that are always served with love. In this chapter, you'll learn how to make comforting Southern entrées that include some of Dolly's personal favorites, such as perfectly crispy Southern Fried Chicken and Southern Chicken and Dumplings. But don't stop at the main course! Choose a couple of side dishes from Chapter 6 and complete the meal with your carb of choice from Chapter 7, like Southern Buttermilk Biscuits or Skillet Cornbread. It's eatin' time!

Country-Fried Steak with White Pepper Gravy

Front Porch Café, Showstreet

Sitting down to supper at the Front Porch Café feels like visiting your Mamaw's house on a Saturday afternoon. Try serving this dish over a bed of Creamy Mashed Potatoes (without the Brown Gravy; see recipe in Chapter 6) with some simple buttered corn and a Garlic Cheddar Biscuit (see recipe in Chapter 7).

SERVES 4

For Country-Fried Steak

4 (8-ounce) cube steaks, pounded ¼" thick
1½ teaspoons salt
1 teaspoon ground black pepper
1 cup whole milk
2 large eggs
1¼ cups all-purpose flour
⅛ teaspoon cayenne pepper
¾ teaspoon paprika
1 teaspoon onion powder
½ teaspoon garlic powder
1 cup canola oil

For White Pepper Gravy

4 tablespoons (½ stick) unsalted butter
¼ cup all-purpose flour
2½ cups whole milk
2 teaspoons ground black pepper
¾ teaspoon salt

1. **To make Country-Fried Steak:** Pat steaks dry with paper towels and season both sides with salt and pepper.
2. In a shallow container with a wide bottom, whisk milk with eggs. In a second shallow container with a wide bottom, stir together flour, cayenne pepper, paprika, onion powder, and garlic powder. Dredge a steak in flour mixture on both sides, shake off excess, then dip both sides in egg mixture, letting excess drip back into container. Dredge once more in flour mixture and place on a clean work surface. Repeat with remaining steaks.
3. **Fry Method:** In a large cast iron skillet fitted with a thermometer, add oil ¼" deep and set over medium heat. Heat oil to 375°F. Working in batches, fry steaks 6 minutes or until golden brown and cooked through, flipping halfway through. Transfer to a large plate lined with paper towels.
4. **Oven Method:** Preheat oven to 400°F. Place an oven-safe metal rack over a large baking sheet and spray generously with cooking spray. Place coated steaks on rack and spray flour coating lightly with cooking spray. Bake 12 minutes, flip steaks, and bake 10 more minutes or until golden brown and cooked through.

continued on next page

5. **To make White Pepper Gravy:** In a medium saucepan over medium-low heat, melt butter. Sprinkle flour onto butter and whisk to form a paste. Increase heat to medium and drizzle in milk while whisking constantly to prevent lumps.
6. Add pepper and salt to pan and continue whisking occasionally until gravy has thickened, about 5 minutes. Spoon over Country-Fried Steak and serve.

Southern Fried Chicken

Aunt Granny's Restaurant, Rivertown Junction

If there's one dish that defines Southern cuisine, this is it. The seasoned crunch enrobing pieces of juicy chicken goes well with any comfort food side dish from buttermilk biscuits and mashed potatoes to turnip greens and pinto beans. Dolly Parton's mama made fried chicken on special occasions, and it remains one of Dolly's favorite dishes to this day. As a dinner treat that's hard to resist, it's no surprise that it's also a favorite at Dollywood restaurants, especially as part of the buffet feast at Aunt Granny's.

SERVES 6

1 (5-pound) whole chicken
1 cup buttermilk
2 tablespoons salt, divided
½ cup cornstarch
3 large eggs, beaten
2 cups all-purpose flour
1 tablespoon ground black pepper
1 tablespoon garlic powder
1 teaspoon paprika
½ teaspoon cayenne pepper
1 quart canola oil (for fry method)

1. Pat chicken dry. Use a sharp knife to cut off each drumstick with thigh attached by cutting through skin on each side, then cutting between joints. Cut thigh and drumstick apart by cutting right behind the line of fat nearest the drumstick. Cut wings off by cutting through skin on each side, then cutting between joints. Use kitchen shears to make a cut along each side of backbone and discard. Use knife to cut breastbone into two pieces. You should have eight pieces of chicken.
2. In a gallon-sized zip-top bag, combine buttermilk and 1 tablespoon salt. Add chicken pieces, seal bag, and shake to coat. Refrigerate 2 hours.
3. In a shallow container with a wide bottom, add cornstarch. In a second shallow container with a wide bottom, add eggs. In a third shallow container with a wide bottom, stir together flour, remaining 1 tablespoon salt, pepper, garlic powder, paprika, and cayenne.
4. Remove chicken from marinade and pat dry. Lightly coat each piece in cornstarch and shake off excess. Then dip each piece into beaten eggs, letting excess drip back into container. Finally, dip each piece into flour mixture, making sure it is generously coated on both sides.

continued on next page

5. **Fry Method:** In a large cast iron skillet fitted with a thermometer, add oil 1½" deep and set over medium heat. Heat oil to 350°F. Being careful not to crowd the pan, fry chicken pieces while turning every 2 minutes until cooked to an internal temperature of 165°F. Fry time will vary between 10 and 20 minutes depending on thickness and type of meat. Transfer chicken to a large plate lined with paper towels to drain.
6. **Oven Method:** Preheat oven to 425°F. Place an oven-safe metal rack over a large baking sheet and spray generously with cooking spray. Arrange chicken pieces on rack, leaving space between each one. Lightly spray flour coating with cooking spray. Roast 30 minutes, use a metal spatula to turn chicken pieces, and roast an additional 12 minutes or just until cooked to an internal temperature of 165°F. Some pieces will cook faster than others—remove finished pieces from the oven as they reach the proper temperature.

Did You Know?

You can also find fried chicken at Miss Lillian's Smokehouse in Craftsman's Valley or at Song & Hearth at Dollywood's DreamMore Resort & Spa.

Fried Catfish (photo on next page)

Aunt Granny's Restaurant, Rivertown Junction

Fried catfish is believed to have originated from West African people who brought their culinary traditions with them to the United States. Catfish were found in abundance in Southern lakes and rivers of the United States and were easy to prepare over a fire right after the fish were caught. Later considered a staple of soul food cuisine when the term was popularized in the 1960s, this well-seasoned and delightfully crunchy fish remains a top pick for Southern plates as well as visitors to Dollywood.

SERVES 4

1 cup buttermilk
4 (4-ounce) catfish fillets
½ cup finely ground yellow cornmeal
1 tablespoon Cajun seasoning
½ teaspoon lemon pepper seasoning
½ teaspoon garlic powder
½ teaspoon salt
½ teaspoon ground black pepper
2 cups canola oil (for fry method)

1. Add buttermilk to a wide, shallow container. Pat catfish dry with a paper towel, add to buttermilk, turning once to coat, and let sit while preparing other ingredients.
2. In a second wide, shallow container, add cornmeal, Cajun seasoning, lemon pepper, garlic powder, salt, and pepper. Lift a catfish fillet out of buttermilk, letting excess drip back into container. Dredge in cornmeal mixture on both sides, shake off excess, then set onto a clean work surface. Repeat with remaining fillets.
3. **Fry Method:** In a large cast iron skillet fitted with a thermometer, add oil ½" deep and set over medium-high heat. Heat oil to 365°F. Working in batches if needed, fry catfish 6 minutes or until golden and crispy and cooked to an internal temperature of 145°F, turning once halfway through. Transfer catfish to a large plate lined with paper towels to drain 2 minutes.
4. **Oven Method:** Preheat oven to 400°F. Place an oven-safe metal rack over a large baking sheet and spray generously with cooking spray. Arrange catfish on rack and spray coating lightly with cooking spray. Bake 20 minutes or until catfish flakes easily with a fork and reaches an internal temperature of 145°F.

Chicken Cassoulet

Granny Ogle's Ham 'n' Beans, Craftsman's Valley

Cassoulet is a dish originating from France that consists of white beans slow-cooked with herbs, vegetables, and a variety of meats. Sometimes a crust of breadcrumbs, dumplings, and/or cheese is added to the cassoulet and baked in the oven before serving. Dollywood's take on this meal uses fresh herbs to season smoked sausage, chicken, and an aromatic combination of vegetables. Served in a personal-sized cast iron skillet, this bestselling dish gives legume lovers something to smile about.

SERVES 4

- 6 pieces thick-sliced bacon, chopped
- 4 medium cloves garlic, peeled and minced
- 1 cup diced white onion
- 1 cup diced celery
- 2 cups sliced smoked sausage
- 2 cups chopped cooked chicken breast and thighs
- 3 bay leaves
- 1 sprig fresh rosemary
- 1 teaspoon ground black pepper
- ½ teaspoon salt
- 2 teaspoons spicy mustard
- 1 cup chicken stock
- 1 cup sliced and peeled carrots
- 1 cup halved cherry tomatoes
- 2 (15.5 ounce) cans cannellini beans, drained, unrinsed

1. In a Dutch oven or medium pot over medium heat, add bacon. Let cook, stirring occasionally, 3 minutes or until bacon starts to release its juices. Add garlic, onion, and celery and cook 4 minutes while stirring occasionally.
2. Add sausage, chicken, bay leaves, rosemary, pepper, salt, mustard, stock, carrots, tomatoes, and beans to pot. Stir, place lid on pot, and reduce heat to low. Cook 30 minutes, stirring occasionally. Remove and discard rosemary sprig and bay leaves before serving.

Meatloaf Stackers

Granny Ogle's Ham 'n' Beans, Craftsman's Valley

There's little to not love about a thick slice of butter-infused white bread, a hearty chunk of Dollywood's famous meatloaf, and a mighty scoop of creamy mashed potatoes all piled on top of each other and finished off with a ladle of flavorful brown gravy. Typical park sides are cole slaw, pinto beans, and cornbread.

SERVES 4

1 pound ground chuck
½ cup finely chopped yellow onion
1 medium clove garlic, peeled and minced
¼ cup finely chopped red bell pepper
¼ cup finely chopped green bell pepper
1 large egg
1 tablespoon Worcestershire sauce
¾ teaspoon salt
1¼ teaspoons ground black pepper
¾ cup plain breadcrumbs
¾ cup ketchup
3 tablespoons yellow mustard
1½ tablespoons packed light brown sugar
4 slices Butter Crust Bread (see recipe in Chapter 7)
½ recipe Creamy Mashed Potatoes and Brown Gravy (see recipe in Chapter 6)

1. Preheat oven to 350°F. Spray a loaf pan with nonstick cooking spray and set aside.
2. In a large bowl, add ground chuck, onion, garlic, bell peppers, egg, Worcestershire sauce, salt, black pepper, and breadcrumbs. Use clean hands to mix ingredients until fully combined. Press mixture into loaf pan.
3. In a small bowl, whisk ketchup, mustard, and brown sugar until sugar starts to dissolve. Spread sauce on top of meatloaf.
4. Cover pan with aluminum foil and bake on center rack 35 minutes, then uncover and bake an additional 20 minutes or until meatloaf reaches an internal temperature of 160°F.
5. Serve on slices of Butter Crust Bread and top with Creamy Mashed Potatoes and Brown Gravy.

Pit Ham

Granny Ogle's Ham 'n' Beans, Craftsman's Valley

Did you know that the name "pit ham" doesn't have anything to do with a smoking pit? It's an anagram for "partially internally trimmed," which means that the ham has had the bone and some fat removed before being tied back together and smoked. The meat is relatively lean and deliciously tender, making it the perfect star of a traditional ham dinner or sliced up in sandwiches. Staying true to the name of the restaurant itself, pit ham is served with Granny Ogle's Pinto Beans (see recipe in Chapter 6).

SERVES 10

- 1 (7-pound) precooked pit ham
- 1 cup warm water (110°F)
- ½ cup packed light brown sugar
- ½ cup pure maple syrup
- 1 teaspoon liquid smoke
- 2 tablespoons Dijon mustard
- ¼ teaspoon ground allspice

1. Preheat oven to 350°F.
2. Pat ham dry with paper towels and use a sharp knife to score the outside in a diamond pattern. Place ham in a large roasting pan and add enough of the water to reach a depth of ¼". Roast until ham has an internal temperature of 140°F, about 70 minutes (10 minutes per pound).
3. While ham is roasting, prepare glaze: In a medium saucepan over medium-low heat, combine brown sugar, maple syrup, liquid smoke, mustard, and allspice. Stir frequently until sugar fully dissolves, about 5 minutes. If glaze is too thick, stir in warm water a teaspoon at a time until it is the consistency of a thin syrup. Keep warm.
4. Brush glaze onto ham during the last 20 minutes of roasting, and watch it closely to ensure it does not burn. Let ham rest on counter 30 minutes before serving.

Smoke It

If you want to double-smoke your ham, omit liquid smoke from the glaze and set your smoker to 225°F. Smoke ham until it reaches an internal temperature of 135°F, about 10 minutes per pound. Brush on glaze, reapplying every 10 minutes. Continue smoking until internal temperature reaches 140°F. Lightly cover with aluminum foil and let ham rest for 30 minutes before serving.

Pot Roast

Granny Ogle's Ham 'n' Beans, Craftsman's Valley

While Granny Ogle's is most famous for their bean-centric recipes, their deliciously tender pot roast is not something to miss. The beef is cooked to perfection and practically melts in your mouth. It is served with a thickened sauce made from the roast's own cooking juices. The use of fresh herbs, onions, and a long, slow roast gives this dish its incredible texture and flavor. Enjoy this meal on a chilly winter night for the full experience.

SERVES 10

- 1 tablespoon olive oil
- 1½ teaspoons salt
- 1½ teaspoons ground black pepper
- 1 (4-pound) chuck roast
- 3 cups beef stock, divided
- 1 large yellow onion, peeled and cut into large chunks
- 2 sprigs fresh thyme
- 2 sprigs fresh rosemary
- 1 tablespoon cornstarch

1. Preheat oven to 275°F.
2. Heat oil in a large Dutch oven over medium-high heat. Rub salt and pepper generously onto top and bottom of roast.
3. Sear roast 1 minute on each side, then remove to a large plate. Add 2 tablespoons stock to Dutch oven and use a spatula to deglaze the bottom (scrape up the flavorful bits).
4. Return roast to Dutch oven and pack onion around edges. Add remaining stock until it reaches halfway up roast, then top with sprigs of thyme and rosemary.
5. Place lid on Dutch oven and transfer to oven. Roast 1 hour per pound of beef, about 4 hours or until roast is extremely tender and falls apart when pulled with a fork.
6. When roast is done, use two sturdy spatulas to transfer to a platter. Discard rosemary and thyme. Strain remaining juices from Dutch oven to a small saucepan set over medium heat. Whisk in cornstarch, stirring continuously, and cook until bubbling and thick, about 3 minutes. Serve over roast.

Did You Know?

When a beef roast is cooked and served with root vegetables such as carrots and potatoes, it is known as a Yankee Pot Roast.

Creamy Vegetable Soup

Dolly Parton's Stampede

Dolly Parton's Stampede Dinner Attraction features a grand four-course feast that guests enjoy during an exuberant show with horse riders wearing costumes, pyrotechnics, and some lighthearted competition. While all of the food served up during the dinner is amazing, visitors rave about this unforgettable thick and creamy soup. The soup is so popular that a dried mix is sold at the attraction and online so that guests can re-create their own at home. This recipe is made from scratch, so no mix is required to get the same effect! Go ahead and dunk a hot buttermilk biscuit in it for the full experience—it's just the right thing to do.

SERVES 4

2 large carrots, peeled and finely chopped
1 medium stalk celery, minced
½ cup frozen peas
¼ cup (½ stick) unsalted butter
¼ cup minced white onion
2 medium cloves garlic, peeled and minced
½ teaspoon ground white pepper
1 teaspoon salt
3 tablespoons all-purpose flour
1 cup chicken stock
1 cup whole milk
1 cup heavy cream

1. In a medium stockpot, add carrots and celery. Cover with water and set over medium-high heat. Bring to a low boil 5 minutes. Add peas and boil an additional 5 minutes. Drain through colander and return empty stockpot to stove. Reduce heat to medium-low.
2. Add butter to pot and stir until melted. Add onion and let cook 3 minutes, then add garlic and cook 1 minute more, stirring occasionally. Season with pepper and salt. Sprinkle in flour and whisk until a paste is formed. Add stock while whisking constantly to remove lumps.
3. Let simmer 3 minutes, then drizzle in milk and cream while continuing to whisk constantly.
4. Return drained vegetables to pot and stir. Simmer 15 minutes or until soup has thickened. Serve hot.

Southern Chicken and Dumplings

Song & Hearth: A Southern Eatery, Dollywood's DreamMore Resort & Spa

You don't have to be a guest at Dollywood's DreamMore Resort & Spa to dine at its elaborately decorated restaurant Song & Hearth. Serving breakfast, dinner, and a Sunday brunch, the buffet features a rotating array of classic Southern entrées and side dishes, including one of Dolly's favorites: Chicken and Dumplings! From the flavorful broth to the pillow-like dumplings, this is a meal all by itself, and now you can enjoy it whenever you want.

SERVES 6

1 tablespoon olive oil
1 cup minced yellow onion
½ cup minced celery
1 (64-ounce) box chicken broth
3 cups cooked shredded chicken breast and thighs
½ teaspoon ground black pepper
2½ teaspoons salt, divided
2 cups all-purpose flour
½ teaspoon baking soda
3 tablespoons shortening
¾ cup buttermilk

1. In a large soup pot, heat oil over medium heat. Add onion and celery and sauté 4 minutes or until softened. Add broth, chicken, pepper, and 2 teaspoons salt. Stir, increase heat to high, and bring broth to a boil. Reduce heat to medium-low and allow mixture to simmer.
2. While broth is simmering, prepare dumplings: In a medium mixing bowl, combine flour, baking soda, and remaining ½ teaspoon salt. Cut shortening into dry ingredients using a fork or a pastry cutter until mixture resembles coarse crumbs.
3. Drizzle in buttermilk while stirring until a crumbly dough is formed. Turn mixture out onto a nonstick surface and gently work with hands until ingredients are combined and dough is formed. Press dough out into a rectangle ½" thick. Use a pizza cutter to cut into 1"-square dumplings.
4. Increase heat to medium-high and return broth to a boil. One by one, drop dumplings into broth. Reduce heat to low, cover, and cook 10 minutes. Serve warm.

Dolly's Stone Soup

Song & Hearth: A Southern Eatery, Dollywood's DreamMore Resort & Spa

Dolly Parton said her mama, Avie Lee, was always tuned into the individual needs of her twelve children. She used this soup as a way to both involve her kids in the cooking process and give some special attention to a child that needed a little extra love. While the soup was being prepared, Avie Lee sent her kids outside to each collect a small stone. When the siblings brought their stones inside and gave them to their mom, she chose the "perfect" one—presented by the child she secretly knew needed a boost that day—to wash and toss right into the soup pot! While you don't need to include the stone to make this delicious soup, this is a touching tradition to try with your own family.

SERVES 8

8 cups chicken stock
1 pound russet potatoes, peeled and cut into ½" chunks
1 (14.5-ounce) can diced tomatoes, drained
4 cups chopped cabbage
1 pound turnips, diced
2 large carrots, peeled and diced
⅓ cup chopped sweet onion
4 medium cloves garlic, peeled and minced
1 pound smoked ham hock
1 teaspoon salt
1 teaspoon ground black pepper
1 small clean stone (optional)

1. In a large stockpot over medium heat, add stock, potatoes, tomatoes, cabbage, turnips, carrots, onion, garlic, and ham hock. Season with salt and pepper and stir to combine.
2. Increase heat to medium-high and bring to a boil. Once boiling, reduce heat to medium-low and allow to simmer, stirring occasionally, 2 hours or until vegetables are tender.
3. Remove ham hock and shred meat from bone. Return meat to soup and discard bone. Drop stone into soup, if desired. Serve warm.

Greek Pastitsio

Front Porch Café, Showstreet, Festival of Nations

Also known as Greek lasagna, pastitsio is a layered dish of long tubular pasta with a red meat sauce. The sauce contains a secret ingredient that gives it a little something special: cinnamon! Topped with a creamy béchamel sauce and cheese, there won't be an empty belly in sight after enjoying this for dinner. First appearing during Festival of Nations—the predecessor to Dollywood's Flower & Food Festival—it was a beloved seasonal menu item that was served alongside a Greek salad with feta, cucumbers, and olives.

SERVES 12

For Meat Sauce and Pasta

4 teaspoons olive oil, divided
1 cup finely chopped red onion
3 medium cloves garlic, peeled and minced
2 pounds ground chuck
½ cup beef stock
1 (28-ounce) can crushed tomatoes, including juice
1 cube beef bouillon
2 tablespoons tomato paste
1 teaspoon granulated sugar
1 teaspoon salt
½ teaspoon ground black pepper
1 teaspoon ground cinnamon
1 teaspoon ground oregano
1 teaspoon ground thyme
½ teaspoon paprika
2 bay leaves
1 (16-ounce) box bucatini pasta

1. **To make Meat Sauce and Pasta:** Heat 2 teaspoons oil in a large saucepan over medium heat. Add onion and cook 3 minutes, then add garlic and cook 1 minute more. Add ground chuck, break into small pieces with a spatula, and cook for about 9 minutes or until no pink remains. Drain.
2. To beef mixture, add stock, crushed tomatoes, bouillon, tomato paste, sugar, salt, pepper, cinnamon, oregano, thyme, paprika, and bay leaves. Stir, increase heat to medium-high, and bring to a low boil. Once boiling, reduce heat to medium-low and simmer, uncovered, 45 minutes, while stirring occasionally.
3. While sauce is simmering, cook pasta al dente according to package instructions. Toss with remaining 2 teaspoons oil and let cool 5 minutes. Place in a deep 10" × 15" lasagna pan, arranging pasta so it faces the same direction.

For Béchamel Sauce

½ cup (1 stick) unsalted butter
¾ cup all-purpose flour
¾ teaspoon salt
¼ teaspoon ground black pepper
4 cups whole milk
2 large eggs, lightly beaten
5 ounces pecorino romano cheese, shredded

4. **To make Béchamel Sauce:** Preheat oven to 350°F. In a second large saucepan over medium heat, melt butter. Whisk in flour, salt, and pepper until a paste is formed. Drizzle in milk while whisking constantly to prevent lumps. Bring to a low boil while stirring frequently and cook 3 minutes or until thickened.
5. In a small bowl, add eggs. Whisk in ½ cup hot butter and milk mixture while whisking constantly, then return contents of bowl to saucepan. Cook 3 minutes while stirring. Remove from heat.
6. Pour Meat Sauce evenly over Pasta. Top with Béchamel Sauce, sprinkle with cheese, and bake 30 minutes or until cheese is melted and Béchamel Sauce is bubbly. Let cool 15 minutes before serving.

Substitutions

You can substitute penne pasta for bucatini and Parmesan cheese for pecorino romano.

Mountain Paella

Market Square BIG SKILLET®, Rivertown Junction, Dollywood's Flower & Food Festival

While the traditional version of Spanish paella contains rabbit meat and snails, Dollywood's twist uses a quadruple-punch combination of chicken, shrimp, spicy chorizo, and thin strips of steak.

SERVES 6

8 ounces medium uncooked shrimp, peeled and deveined
8 ounces flank steak, sliced thin
16 ounces boneless, skinless chicken breasts, cut into small cubes
1 teaspoon salt
½ teaspoon ground black pepper
½ teaspoon ground thyme
4 tablespoons olive oil, divided
1 cup finely chopped white onion
1 medium red bell pepper, seeded, cored, and finely chopped
4 medium garlic cloves, peeled and minced
7 ounces chorizo, sliced
3 cups short-grain Valencia rice
4½ cups chicken broth
¾ teaspoon saffron powder
3 tablespoons lemon juice
1 cup frozen peas

1. Season shrimp, steak, and chicken with salt, black pepper, and thyme. Heat 2 tablespoons oil in a wide skillet or paella pan over medium heat. Add onion and bell pepper and cook 3 minutes, then add garlic and cook 1 minute more.
2. Add chicken to skillet and cook 3 minutes while stirring. Add steak and chorizo and cook 3 minutes more, stirring occasionally.
3. Sprinkle rice onto mixture in skillet and cook 2 minutes to toast while stirring constantly. Add broth, saffron, lemon juice, and remaining 2 tablespoons oil. Increase heat to medium-high and bring to a boil. Once boiling, reduce heat to medium-low, cover, and simmer 10 minutes or until rice is tender and has absorbed most of the liquid in skillet.
4. Add peas, stir, and place shrimp on top of mixture. Cover, and cook an additional 5 minutes or until shrimp is cooked through.

Three-Bean Pumpkin Chili

Miss Lillian's BBQ Corner, Craftsman's Valley, Harvest Festival

Dollywood's Harvest Festival was voted America's #1 Fall Family Event by *USA TODAY* readers. The mouthwatering food is a major feature of the festival, and the spectacular autumnal decor is a spectacle as well. This warm and hearty chili is the perfect meal to enjoy while taking in the lights, or to remind you of a crisp Smoky Mountain fall.

SERVES 8

1 tablespoon olive oil
¾ cup finely chopped yellow onion
1 medium yellow bell pepper, seeded, cored, and finely chopped
3 medium garlic cloves, peeled and minced
1 pound ground chuck
3 tablespoons chili powder
1 tablespoon ground cumin
¾ teaspoon ground cinnamon
1 teaspoon salt
½ teaspoon ground black pepper
1 (28-ounce) can crushed tomatoes, including juice
1 (15-ounce) can cannellini beans, drained, unrinsed
1 (15-ounce) can pinto beans, drained, unrinsed
1 (15-ounce) can dark red kidney beans, drained, unrinsed
1 (15-ounce) can pumpkin purée
1 ounce dark chocolate, chopped

1. In a large soup pot, heat oil over medium heat. Add onion and bell pepper. Cook 3 minutes, stirring occasionally, then add garlic and cook 1 minute more. Add ground chuck and break into small pieces with a spatula. Cook 9 minutes or until beef is browned. Drain.
2. Add chili powder, cumin, cinnamon, salt, and black pepper to pot. Stir to combine. Add tomatoes, all beans, and pumpkin. Stir well, bring to a boil over medium-high heat, then reduce heat to medium-low.
3. Simmer uncovered 40 minutes or until chili has thickened, stirring occasionally. Stir in chopped chocolate until melted. Serve warm.

Serving Tip

For a true park re-creation, serve this chili drizzled with avocado crema from the Smoky Mountain Nachos in Chapter 4 and a thick slice of Pumpkin Cornbread from Chapter 7.

Chicken and Andouille Sausage Gumbo with Grits

Front Porch Café, Showstreet, Harvest Festival

This boldly seasoned Creole gumbo is a standout menu item during Dollywood's Harvest Festival. When creating this meal at home, the long simmer time is imperative for allowing the flavors to fully develop. Served with creamy and toothsome grits stirred with melted smoked Gouda, this is the perfect partner for a crisp fall evening.

SERVES 6

For Chicken and Andouille Sausage Gumbo

¼ cup plus 1 tablespoon canola oil, divided
1 pound boneless, skinless chicken thighs, cut into small pieces
14 ounces smoked andouille sausage, sliced
1 cup chopped white onion
1 cup chopped green bell pepper
1 cup chopped celery
2 medium garlic cloves, peeled and minced
1¼ cups sliced okra
6 cups chicken broth
1 (15-ounce) can crushed tomatoes, including juice
2 teaspoons Creole seasoning
½ teaspoon salt
½ teaspoon ground black pepper
2 bay leaves
¼ cup all-purpose flour
1 tablespoon filé powder

1. **To make Chicken and Andouille Sausage Gumbo:** In a medium stockpot, heat 1 tablespoon oil over medium-high heat. Add chicken pieces and sear 2 minutes on each side. Remove to a large plate. Add sliced sausage and sear 1 minute on each side. Remove to plate with chicken.
2. If needed, add an extra teaspoon of oil to pot. Add onion, bell pepper, and celery. Sauté 4 minutes, add garlic, and sauté 1 minute more. Return chicken and sausage to pot along with okra, broth, tomatoes, Creole seasoning, salt, and black pepper. Stir, being sure to scrape up flavorful bits on bottom of pot.
3. Place bay leaves on top and bring to a boil over same heat level, then reduce heat to low. Cover, and cook 2 hours, stirring occasionally.
4. When gumbo is almost done, prepare roux: In a small saucepan, heat remaining ¼ cup oil over medium heat. Whisk in flour until free of lumps and continue whisking constantly, being sure to scrape bottom of pan. If mixture begins to smoke, remove from heat immediately, stir to cool slightly, then return to heat. Remove from heat when mixture forms a deep brown roux, about 20 minutes.

continued on next page

For Smoked Gouda Cheese Grits

6 cups whole milk
½ teaspoon salt
1½ cups 5-minute grits
1 cup shredded smoked Gouda
6 tablespoons unsalted butter
⅓ cup chopped scallions

5. Remove lid from stockpot and discard bay leaves. Stir in roux, increase heat to medium-high, and return to a boil. Once boiling, reduce heat to medium-low and simmer 15 minutes or until thick. Stir in filé powder.
6. **To make Smoked Gouda Cheese Grits:** In a medium saucepan over medium-high heat, bring milk to a boil. Add salt. Slowly add grits while whisking vigorously and constantly to prevent lumps. Reduce heat to medium-low, cover, and cook 5 minutes, stirring occasionally, until thickened.
7. Remove from heat and stir in cheese and butter until melted. Add more salt if desired. Serve alongside gumbo, topped with scallions.

CHAPTER SIX

Southern Sides

Everyone knows that on a plate piled high with comfort food, the side dishes are often the best part! Between Dollywood and its neighboring attractions, you can find just about any Southern side dish in existence. This chapter offers an assortment of the more popular sides at the park, from cold Deviled Eggs and Potato Salad to piping-hot Smoked Mac and Cheese and Roasted Corn cooked right in the husk. Choose a couple recipes to accompany a main dish in Chapter 5, or make a full meal out of different sides. Mix and match vegetables and starches to add color and texture to your plate.

Fried Green Tomatoes

Front Porch Café, Showstreet

At Front Porch Café, these delicious tomatoes are served with a pinch of Parmesan and a little bowl of homemade buttermilk ranch dressing for dipping.

SERVES 5

1 cup all-purpose flour
1 cup self-rising white cornmeal
1 cup seasoned bread crumbs
½ cup buttermilk
2 large eggs
2 teaspoons salt
½ teaspoon ground black pepper
4 medium-sized firm green tomatoes, sliced ½" thick
2 cups canola oil (for fry method)
⅓ cup shredded Parmesan cheese
½ cup ranch dressing

1. In a shallow container with a flat bottom, add flour. In a second shallow container with a flat bottom, add cornmeal and bread crumbs. Stir to combine. In a third shallow container with a flat bottom, stir together buttermilk and eggs. In a pinch bowl, stir together salt and pepper.
2. Generously sprinkle both sides of tomato slices with salt and pepper. Dredge tomatoes in flour until fully coated and shake off excess into container. Next, dip tomatoes in egg and buttermilk mixture, letting excess drip back into container. Finally, dredge tomatoes in cornmeal mixture, making sure both sides are fully coated.
3. **Fry Method:** In a large cast iron skillet fitted with a thermometer, add oil ½" deep and set over medium heat. Heat oil to 360°F. Working in batches, fry tomatoes 2 minutes per side or until golden and crispy. Transfer to a large plate lined with paper towels to drain, keeping slices in a single layer.
4. **Oven Method:** Preheat oven to 375°F. Place an oven-safe wire rack over a baking sheet and spray generously with cooking spray. Arrange the tomato slices on the rack, leaving space between each one. You may need to bake in batches or use multiple baking sheets. Spray cornmeal coating lightly with cooking spray. Bake 15 minutes, use a metal spatula to flip tomatoes, rotate pans if using more than one, then bake an additional 15 minutes or until golden brown. Turn oven to broil on high and broil 2 minutes or until tomatoes are crispy.
5. Sprinkle tomatoes with cheese and serve immediately with ranch dressing on the side for dipping.

Southern-Style Green Beans

Front Porch Café, Showstreet

Front Porch Café was formerly known as Backstage Restaurant before it underwent a major renovation during the off-season in 2017. One dish that remained the same throughout the restaurant's transition is Southern-Style Green Beans, which get their flavor from being cooked with onion, garlic, and, of course, bacon! A staple of Southern cuisine, you can also find green beans at Aunt Granny's Restaurant and Miss Lillian's Smokehouse in the park.

SERVES 4

4 thick-cut slices bacon, chopped
¾ cup diced yellow onion
3 medium cloves garlic, peeled and minced
2 pounds fresh green beans, ends trimmed
3 cups chicken broth
½ teaspoon salt
½ teaspoon ground black pepper

1. In a large sauté pan over medium heat, add bacon and cook 6 minutes or until browned, stirring frequently. Add onion and cook 5 minutes while stirring, then add garlic and cook 1 minute more.
2. Add green beans to pan and stir to combine. Pour in broth, increase heat to medium-high, and bring to a boil. Once boiling, reduce heat to medium-low. Season with salt and pepper and stir.
3. Cover pan and simmer 90 minutes or until beans are tender (start checking after 50 minutes, as overcooked beans will be mushy). Serve using a slotted spoon to strain out chicken broth.

Hot Pimento Cheese Dip

Front Porch Café, Showstreet

Back in 1908, *Good Housekeeping* published one of the first variations of pimento cheese that included cream cheese, mustard, chives, and pimentos. The combination was a huge hit, especially in the South. After World War II, Cheddar cheese and mayonnaise were invited to the party, and the combination exploded in popularity, showing up at everything from family dinners to church potlucks. Front Porch Café's pimento cheese takes this classic chilled appetizer and sandwich filling and turns it into a warm, creamy dip with just the right amount of spice.

SERVES 8

8 ounces cream cheese, room temperature
1 cup mayonnaise
2 (4-ounce) jars diced pimentos, drained
1 teaspoon Worcestershire sauce
2 dashes (¼ teaspoon) hot sauce
½ teaspoon ground black pepper
½ teaspoon salt
⅛ teaspoon cayenne pepper
8 ounces shredded sharp Cheddar cheese
8 ounces shredded pepper jack cheese

1. Preheat oven to 375°F. Spray an 8" × 8" baking dish with nonstick cooking spray.
2. In a large bowl, beat cream cheese with mayonnaise. Add pimentos, Worcestershire, hot sauce, black pepper, salt, and cayenne pepper. Mix to combine.
3. Fold in both cheeses. Spread mixture into prepared baking dish. Bake 15 minutes or until cheese is melted and dip is hot and bubbly.

Serving Tip

The pimento cheese at Front Porch Café is served with homemade crostini or breadsticks. Try this recipe with some barbecue pork rinds for an extra-playful snack!

Creamy Mashed Potatoes and Brown Gravy

Aunt Granny's Restaurant, Rivertown Junction

Dollywood's version of this Southern staple can be found at the buffet at Aunt Granny's (and Miss Lillian's Smokehouse), as well as table service–style at the Front Porch Café and Granny Ogle's Ham 'n' Beans. This recipe is also a main component of the beloved Meatloaf Stackers from Chapter 5. Pair your mashed potatoes and gravy with any of your favorite entrées like fried chicken or pot roast—they go with everything!

SERVES 10

For Creamy Mashed Potatoes

- 5 pounds russet potatoes, peeled, rinsed, and quartered
- 2½ tablespoons salt, divided
- 1¼ cups warm whole milk (110°F)
- ¼ cup warm heavy cream (110°F)
- 1 cup (2 sticks) unsalted butter, softened

For Brown Gravy

- 2 cups beef broth
- 2 cubes beef bouillon
- 4 tablespoons (½ stick) unsalted butter
- ¼ cup all-purpose flour
- ½ teaspoon salt
- ½ teaspoon ground black pepper
- ½ teaspoon onion powder
- ¼ teaspoon ground sage
- ⅛ teaspoon ground thyme

1. **To make Creamy Mashed Potatoes:** Add potato quarters to a large pot and add enough cold water to cover by 1". Add 2 tablespoons salt to water and place over high heat. Bring to a boil, then reduce heat to medium-low and simmer until potatoes are fork-tender, about 25 minutes. Turn off heat, drain potatoes through a colander, and return to warm pot.
2. Add remaining ½ tablespoon salt, milk, heavy cream, and butter to pot. Use a potato masher to mash potatoes until creamy. Be careful not to overwork the potatoes, or they will become gummy. If potatoes are too thick, drizzle in a little extra milk and stir.
3. **To make Brown Gravy:** In a small microwave-safe bowl, add broth and bouillon cubes. Microwave 1 minute, then whisk until cubes dissolve. Microwave in additional 15-second increments if needed until dissolved.
4. In a medium saucepan over medium-low heat, add butter. When melted, whisk in flour until a paste is formed. Season with salt, pepper, onion powder, sage, and thyme. Drizzle in beef broth mixture while whisking constantly to prevent lumps. Continue cooking while stirring frequently until thickened, about 3 minutes. Serve over Creamy Mashed Potatoes.

Turnip Greens

Aunt Granny's Restaurant, Rivertown Junction

Southerners eat all kinds of greens, and the origin of this inexpensive dish in America can be traced back to the use of collard greens by the first African Americans of Jamestown, Virginia, in the early 1600s. Over the years, pots of delicious and nutritious greens (turnip, collard, mustard, chard, or kale) became common Southern fare. A long simmer is vital to achieve a perfectly tender result, and a bit of baking soda added at the end helps counteract the natural bitterness of the greens. Try adding a few dashes of hot sauce when serving for some extra pizzazz!

SERVES 6

- 2½ pounds turnip greens
- 1 pound thick-cut hickory-smoked bacon, chopped
- 1 cup finely chopped yellow onion
- 2 medium cloves garlic, peeled and minced
- 1 (14-ounce) can chicken broth
- ¾ cup water
- 3 drops liquid smoke
- 1½ teaspoons salt
- 1 teaspoon ground black pepper
- ½ teaspoon baking soda

1. Place a colander in sink and add greens. Rinse several times with cold water while tossing greens until no sand or grit can be seen or felt. Transfer greens to cutting board and pat dry. Cut off stems, discard, then cut leaves into 1" pieces.
2. Place a large stockpot over medium heat. Add bacon and cook 6 minutes or until browned, stirring frequently. Add onion, stir, cook 4 minutes, then add garlic and cook 1 minute more.
3. Add broth, water, liquid smoke, salt, and pepper. Stir. Add greens to pot, reduce heat to medium-low, cover, and simmer 1 hour.
4. Stir in baking soda. Continue simmering an additional 30 minutes or until greens are very tender. Serve.

Cornbread Dressing

Aunt Granny's Restaurant, Rivertown Junction

Made from repurposed stale cornbread (another Southern staple) mixed with fats, veggies, and spices, cornbread dressing is a recurrent player at Thanksgiving or Sunday supper tables in the South. For best results, let the cornbread and white bread sit out for a day or two to dry out. Doing so will allow the bread to absorb more of the broth and eggs and result in a dressing that's perfectly moist.

SERVES 10

4 tablespoons (½ stick) unsalted butter
1 large yellow onion, peeled and finely chopped
3 medium celery stalks, minced
1 recipe Skillet Cornbread (see recipe in Chapter 7)
4 slices white bread, toasted or stale, diced small
3¼ cups chicken stock, divided
2 large eggs
1 teaspoon salt
1 teaspoon ground black pepper
1 teaspoon poultry seasoning
1½ teaspoons ground sage

1. Preheat oven to 350°F. Spray a 9" × 13" metal pan with nonstick cooking spray and set aside.
2. In a large skillet over medium heat, melt butter. Add onion and celery; stir to coat. Sauté 10 minutes or until vegetables are softened. Remove from heat and transfer to a large mixing bowl. Do not drain.
3. Crumble cornbread and add to bowl with onion and celery. Add white bread, 3 cups stock, eggs, salt, pepper, poultry seasoning, and sage. Use a large wooden spoon to stir and fold mixture until bread is saturated with wet ingredients. If mixture appears dry, stir in remaining ¼ cup stock—it should be wet but not soggy. Add extra if needed.
4. Transfer mixture to prepared pan and bake 35 minutes or until center has set and dressing is golden on top.

Oven-Roasted Red Bliss Potatoes

Aunt Granny's Restaurant, Rivertown Junction

When Dollywood opened in May 1986, it caused quite the traffic jam! As oceans of people crowded into Pigeon Forge to experience the brand-new park, vehicles jammed up Highway 441 for 6 miles. While the cozy setting, fantastic live performances, and thrilling rides are strong draws for visitors, the food also ranks at the tippy-top of the favorites lists. These flavor-loaded red potatoes are one such revered dish and are the perfect complement to any main meal. Skip the bacon and cheese toppings if they aren't your style.

SERVES 4

1½ pounds red potatoes, cut into wedges
1 tablespoon olive oil
½ teaspoon garlic powder
½ teaspoon onion powder
1 teaspoon dried rosemary
½ teaspoon salt
½ teaspoon ground black pepper
2 teaspoons finely chopped fresh parsley
6 slices bacon, cooked crisp and crumbled
½ cup shredded Cheddar cheese

1. Preheat oven to 400°F. Line a large rimmed baking sheet with aluminum foil and set aside.
2. In a large bowl, add potato wedges. In a small bowl, stir together oil, garlic powder, onion powder, rosemary, salt, pepper, and parsley. Drizzle oil mixture over potatoes and toss until fully coated.
3. Transfer potatoes to prepared sheet and use a nonstick spatula to scrape bowl and get all of the flavorings onto potatoes.
4. Roast 30 minutes, stirring and turning the potatoes halfway through cooking. If potatoes are not done, roast an additional 5 minutes or until tender and browned.
5. Remove baking sheet from oven and top potatoes with bacon and cheese. Return to oven 3 minutes or just until cheese is melted.

Corn Pudding

Aunt Granny's Restaurant, Rivertown Junction

Have you noticed the strange-looking wooden clock with a water wheel in Rivertown Junction? The water that keeps the wheel in motion starts at the top of Craftsman's Valley and flows all the way down the hill to the clock. After you admire this lovely feature of Dollywood, head over to Aunt Granny's and see if their Corn Pudding is on the day's menu. Or, better yet, skip the anticipation and enjoy this recipe at home whenever you want! This side dish is hard to stop eating—it is that good. The texture is creamy and structured at the same time. The extra bite from whole corn kernels and creamed corn adds interest along with bold flavor from yellow cornmeal and tang from sour cream.

SERVES 6

1 cup finely ground yellow cornmeal
1 teaspoon baking powder
⅓ cup granulated sugar
1 cup canned creamed corn
1 cup canned yellow corn kernels, drained
2 large eggs
½ cup (1 stick) unsalted butter, melted
1 cup sour cream
½ teaspoon salt
¼ teaspoon ground black pepper

1. Preheat oven to 350°F. Spray a 9" × 9" baking dish with nonstick cooking spray and set aside.
2. In a large bowl, combine cornmeal, baking powder, sugar, creamed corn, corn kernels, eggs, butter, sour cream, salt, and pepper. Pour mixture into prepared pan and spread out evenly using a nonstick spatula.
3. Bake 30 minutes or just until center is set and lightly golden on top. Remove pan from oven 1 minute before pudding looks fully done so it stays moist.

Substitutions

You can use leftover fresh creamed corn or yellow corn in place of canned. You can also use frozen; just let it thaw before mixing it into the pudding.

Honey-Glazed Carrots

Aunt Granny's Restaurant, Rivertown Junction

The side options at Aunt Granny's Restaurant are always rotating, and you never know which ones you will see on the menu. These simple glazed carrots make frequent appearances and are incredibly easy to re-create. The brown sugar and honey highlight the natural sweetness in the carrots, resulting in a versatile dish that pairs well with any entrée.

SERVES 4

1 pound peeled carrots, cut into ¼" slices
2 cups water
2 tablespoons unsalted butter
1 teaspoon packed light brown sugar
2 tablespoons amber honey

1. In a large sauté pan over medium-high heat, add carrots and water, adding more water if carrots are not covered. Bring to a boil, then reduce heat to medium-low. Simmer 6 minutes, then drain.
2. Add butter, brown sugar, and honey to pan. Stir to coat. Simmer 4 more minutes, stirring occasionally, until sugar has dissolved and carrots are tender.

Did You Know?

You may never see any recycling bins at Dollywood, but it's not because of a lack of care for the environment. Sevier County has a robust recycling and composting program that processes 70 percent of all incoming waste. The facility itself separates recyclables from trash and removes the need for presorting. The park makes other efforts to be environmentally friendly as well, such as using paper straws instead of plastic.

Cinnamon Apples

Aunt Granny's Restaurant, Rivertown Junction

Cooked, spiced apples are like the filling of your granny's warm apple pie, just without the crust. The best part of Cinnamon Apples is that you don't have to wait for dessert to eat them—they can be found as a side dish right beside your meat and veggies. Don't wait to try these apples at Aunt Granny's Restaurant: Whip up this easy stovetop version in minutes.

SERVES 6

2 tablespoons unsalted butter
2 tablespoons water
2 tablespoons packed light brown sugar
1 teaspoon pure maple syrup
½ teaspoon pure vanilla extract
¾ teaspoon ground cinnamon
⅛ teaspoon salt
4 medium sweet apples, peeled, cored, and cut into ½" slices

1. In a medium saucepan over medium heat, melt butter. Add water, brown sugar, maple syrup, vanilla, cinnamon, and salt. While stirring, cook 3 minutes or until sugar dissolves. Add apple slices and stir to coat.
2. Reduce heat to low and cover pan. Cook until apples are tender, stirring occasionally, about 15 minutes. Serve warm.

Fried Okra

Aunt Granny's Restaurant, Rivertown Junction

Dolly Parton never had any children of her own, but she has fifteen nieces and nephews who have an affectionate name for her: Aunt Granny! It's no surprise that the buffet restaurant in Craftsman's Valley was named for this beloved moniker. Crunchy fried okra is an all-around hit on Aunt Granny's menu. The key to keeping your okra firm is twofold: Make sure it is dried really well before applying buttermilk and breading, and watch the oil temperature closely to make sure it's not too hot or too cool. You want the okra to fry up fast but not burn.

SERVES 4

1 pound fresh okra, patted dry, ends discarded, cut into ½"-thick slices
½ cup buttermilk
1¼ cups yellow cornmeal
3 tablespoons all-purpose flour
1 teaspoon salt
½ teaspoon ground black pepper
2 cups canola oil

1. Add okra and buttermilk to a gallon-sized zip-top bag, seal, and shake gently to coat.
2. In a large bowl, stir together cornmeal, flour, salt, and pepper. Strain okra from buttermilk and add to dry mixture. Use clean hands to toss okra until fully coated.
3. To a large cast iron skillet fitted with a thermometer over medium heat, add oil ¾" deep and heat to 375°F.
4. Strain okra from dry mixture and fry in oil, working if batches if needed, 3 minutes or until golden brown, turning halfway through. Transfer to a large plate lined with paper towels to drain, 2 minutes.

Tater Twirls

Dogs N Taters, Rivertown Junction

Dollywood's signature Tater Twirls are unlike any curly fries you've had before. After taking your steaming-hot basket to one of the outdoor tables surrounding the walk-up Dogs N Taters snack stand, you might notice that the shape of the fries varies throughout. Some are long and curly, while others are thin and flat, but all of them are equally seasoned and fried to a golden crisp. To fully re-create the park experience, serve this dish alongside a famous Dogs N Taters Footlong Corn Dog (see recipe in Chapter 4).

SERVES 4

- 2 large russet potatoes, scrubbed
- 6¼ cups cold water, divided
- 1¼ cups all-purpose flour
- ¼ cup white cornmeal
- 3½ teaspoons salt, divided
- 2 tablespoons paprika
- 1½ teaspoons onion powder
- 1 teaspoon garlic powder
- ¼ teaspoon cayenne pepper
- 1 teaspoon ground black pepper
- 1 teaspoon granulated sugar
- 1 quart canola oil

1. Fit a stand mixer with spiralizer attachment using small core spiral slice blade (or use a freestanding spiralizer). Spiralize one potato. Switch to medium spiralizer blade and spiralize second potato. Using kitchen shears, snip spirals into 4" sections.
2. Place spiralized potatoes into a large bowl and cover with 5 cups cold water, making sure water completely covers potatoes. Let stand 30 minutes, then drain and pat dry.
3. In a medium bowl, stir together flour, cornmeal, 2½ teaspoons salt, paprika, onion powder, garlic powder, cayenne pepper, black pepper, and sugar. Add remaining 1¼ cups water and stir to form a batter.
4. To a wide sauté pan fitted with a thermometer over medium heat, add oil 2" deep and heat to 350°F.
5. Place a metal oven rack over a large baking sheet. Dip small handfuls of potatoes into batter, let excess drip back into bowl, then transfer to rack.
6. Working in batches and being careful not to crowd pan, fry potatoes 4 minutes or just until golden and crispy. Transfer to a large plate lined with paper towels and immediately season with remaining 1 teaspoon salt.

Smoked Mac and Cheese

Miss Lillian's Smokehouse, Craftsman's Valley

Every Sunday, the Robert F. Thomas Chapel in Craftsman's Valley—named for the doctor who delivered Dolly Parton—hosts a church service. The old-fashioned single-room building with its hardwood flooring and wooden pews gives visitors a true country experience for their Sunday worship. Afterward, Miss Lillian's Smokehouse is just a short stroll down the pathway and is an ideal stop for a delicious Sunday lunch that *must* include this ooey-gooey macaroni and cheese infused with smoky flavor. When making this at home, opt for shredding the cheese fresh off the block (instead of using bags of pre-shredded cheese) for the creamiest result.

SERVES 8

1 pound uncooked elbow macaroni
¼ cup (½ stick) unsalted butter
¼ cup all-purpose flour
2¼ cups whole milk
1 cup sour cream
3 cups shredded smoked Cheddar cheese
8 ounces Velveeta cheese, cut into 1" cubes
4 ounces fresh smoked mozzarella, cut into 1" cubes
1 teaspoon salt
½ teaspoon ground black pepper
½ teaspoon ground mustard
½ teaspoon onion powder
¼ teaspoon smoked paprika

1. Cook macaroni according to package directions and drain in a colander.
2. In a large pot over medium heat, melt butter. Sprinkle in flour and whisk to form a paste. Slowly add milk while whisking constantly to prevent lumps. Let cook 4 minutes or until mixture has thickened.
3. Reduce heat to medium-low, and add sour cream, cheddar, Velveeta, and mozzarella. Stir constantly 3 minutes or until cheese melts and mixture is creamy. Season with salt, pepper, ground mustard, onion powder, and paprika. Stir to combine.
4. Add macaroni to cheese mixture and stir until fully incorporated.
5. Let cook an additional 5 minutes, stirring occasionally, until macaroni is warmed through. (Smoker Method: Warm this dish in an actual smoker for a true park re-creation. Choose mild wood chips like maple, cherry, or pecan. Use a grill-safe pan and smoke at 225°F for about 1 hour.)

Potato Salad

Miss Lillian's Smokehouse, Craftsman's Valley

Despite being the driving force behind one of the best theme parks in the country, Dolly Parton absolutely will not ride the rides! The entertainer suffers from motion sickness and has a fear of roller coasters. While Dolly might not be big on rides, she is big on homestyle Southern food, like a big bowl of this Potato Salad perfectly seasoned and dressed with mustard, sweet relish, and more.

SERVES 8

3 pounds russet potatoes, peeled and cut into 1" cubes
2 tablespoons plus 1 teaspoon salt, divided
4 large eggs, hard-boiled, peeled, and chopped
2 medium stalks celery, finely chopped
¾ cup mayonnaise
1 teaspoon yellow mustard
3 tablespoons sweet relish
1 teaspoon apple cider vinegar
½ teaspoon garlic powder
½ teaspoon ground black pepper

1. In a large pot, add potatoes and enough water to cover by 1". Sprinkle in 2 tablespoons salt and stir gently. Set over high heat and bring to a boil.
2. Once boiling, reduce heat to medium-low and let simmer 10 minutes or until tender when pierced with a fork. Avoid overcooking potatoes, or they will become mealy and mushy. Strain with a colander, let cool 5 minutes, then add to a large bowl with eggs and celery.
3. In a medium bowl, mix together mayonnaise, remaining 1 teaspoon salt, mustard, relish, vinegar, garlic powder, and pepper. Add to potatoes and fold gently to combine, being careful not to mash up potatoes.
4. If potato salad is dry, fold in extra mayonnaise 1 tablespoon at a time. For best flavor, refrigerate 4 hours before serving to allow flavors to meld together.

Roasted Corn

Miss Lillian's BBQ Corner, Craftsman's Valley

Miss Lillian, aka "The Chicken Lady," is a beloved character at Dollywood. She can be found outside of her restaurants, Miss Lillian's Smokehouse and the adjacent Miss Lillian's BBQ Corner, wearing flamboyant outfits, playing her banjo, and interacting with guests. Not only home to one of Dollywood's friendliest faces, this little corner of the park also offers up some tasty food whether you want to sit down or grab and go. This simply prepared corn is roasted right in the husks and doesn't need anything besides some butter, salt, and pepper to be delicious—convenient for eating on the run!

SERVES 6

6 medium ears sweet corn, in husks
3 tablespoons unsalted butter, room temperature
1 teaspoon salt
½ teaspoon ground black pepper

1. Preheat oven to 350°F.
2. Place corn directly on center rack. Roast 30 minutes.
3. Peel back husks and remove silks. Rub with butter, then sprinkle with salt and pepper.

Granny Ogle's Pinto Beans

Granny Ogle's Ham 'n' Beans, Craftsman's Valley

The ham-seasoned pinto beans on Granny Ogle's menu are favored for a reason: This is quintessential Southern comfort food! Serve them up with a thick wedge of Skillet Cornbread (see recipe in Chapter 7), and you'll want to make this dish again and again. And the next time you are dining at Granny Ogle's, keep your ears open; you might hear the energetic beat of country music performers coming from the Valley Theater next door. The sign above the restaurant promises "Country Cookin' At Its Best," and, boy, does it deliver.

SERVES 6

1 pound dry pinto beans
1 tablespoon olive oil
1 medium white onion, peeled and finely chopped
3 medium cloves garlic, peeled and minced
1 pound ham hock
2 (14-ounce) cans vegetable broth
8 ounces cooked ham, shredded
1½ teaspoons salt
1 teaspoon ground black pepper

1. Place dry beans in a large pot and cover with 3" water. Soak 6 hours up to overnight. Drain and rinse beans and clean pot.
2. Heat oil in same pot over medium-high heat. Add onion and stir to coat with oil. Sauté until soft and fragrant, about 5 minutes. Add garlic, stir, and cook 1 minute more.
3. Add beans, ham hock, broth, and enough water to cover mixture with 2" liquid.
4. Bring to a boil, then reduce heat to medium-low. Place lid on pot and simmer 2½ hours or until beans are tender. Check them occasionally and stir to make sure they aren't sticking to the bottom.
5. Once beans are tender, remove ham hock and cut away meat, discarding fat and bones. Return meat to pot; add shredded ham, salt, and pepper. Stir and cook an additional 10 minutes.

Fun Fact

Granny Ogle's was named after the grandmother of one of Dolly Parton's childhood best friends, Judy Ogle.

Deviled Eggs

Granny Ogle's Ham 'n' Beans, Craftsman's Valley

Craftsman's Valley is home to Eagle Mountain Sanctuary, Dollywood's 30,000-square-foot aviary that protects the country's largest collection of bald eagles that cannot be returned to the wild. In operation since 1990, the sanctuary has also bred and released more than 160 bald eagles into the Smoky Mountains. After learning about these beautiful birds of prey, you might have eggs on the brain! Just down the pathway from the sanctuary is Granny Ogle's, where you can start your meal with these classic Deviled Eggs finished with a plethora of creative toppings.

SERVES 4

6 large eggs
¼ cup mayonnaise
1 teaspoon dill pickle juice
1 teaspoon yellow mustard
⅛ teaspoon salt
⅛ teaspoon ground black pepper

1. Place eggs into a medium pot and add enough cold water to cover by 1". Place over high heat and bring to a boil. Boil 1 minute, then turn off heat. Cover pot and let sit 12 minutes.
2. Gently pour out hot water, then run cold water over eggs. Let sit 5 minutes. Crack shells and peel eggs carefully, rinse off any excess shell pieces, and pat dry with paper towels. Slice eggs in half and transfer yolks to a medium bowl. Place egg whites on a large plate.
3. To yolks, add mayonnaise, pickle juice, mustard, salt, and pepper. Use a fork to mash yolks and stir until creamy. Spoon filling into egg whites.

Serving Tip

Granny Ogle's serves their deviled eggs plain or topped with a combo of crumbled bacon, ham, shredded Cheddar cheese, or chopped scallions. Try this recipe with a sprinkle of smoked paprika for a more traditional variety.

Candied Sweet Potato Soufflé

Song & Hearth: A Southern Eatery, Dollywood's DreamMore Resort & Spa

The grand buffet room at DreamMore's elaborate dining establishment is any food lover's fantasy. The Candied Sweet Potato Soufflé often served on the smorgasbord consists of sweetened whipped sweet potatoes baked with a buttery brown sugar–pecan topping. The chefs at Song & Hearth bake their soufflé in a cast iron skillet, though you can use any metal or ceramic baking dish you have on hand.

SERVES 8

6 medium sweet potatoes
½ cup whole milk
¾ cup granulated sugar
1½ teaspoons salt
1 tablespoon pure vanilla extract
2 large eggs
1 cup packed dark brown sugar
⅓ cup all-purpose flour
⅓ cup unsalted butter, melted
1 cup chopped pecans

1. Preheat oven to 400°F. Line a large baking sheet with parchment paper.
2. Use a fork to pierce potatoes on all sides and place on prepared sheet. Bake 50 minutes or until centers are very soft when pierced with a knife.
3. Remove potatoes from oven and reduce temperature to 350°F. Use a knife to slice open potatoes to allow steam to escape. Let cool on baking sheet 10 minutes.
4. Scoop insides of potatoes into a large bowl. Whip with hand mixer until smooth. Add milk, granulated sugar, salt, and vanilla. Mix on low speed until ingredients are fully incorporated. Add eggs one at a time, mixing after each addition until combined. Pour potato mixture into a large cast iron skillet (do not preheat skillet in oven).
5. In a medium bowl, mix brown sugar, flour, butter, and pecans. Sprinkle on top of potatoes. Bake on center rack 40 minutes or until topping is browned.

CHAPTER SEVEN

Lovin' from the Oven

Prepare to be covered in flour, because this chapter is all about the entrancing baked goods and desserts that Dollywood hosts produce every single day. In this chapter, you'll learn how to make breads using a variety of leavening agents, biscuits with both cold and melted butter (the difference matters!), flaky pie crust from scratch, and laminated pastry dough. You'll also discover easy recipes for Dolly's favorite desserts, like banana pudding and peach cobbler. Whether you need a sweet breakfast pastry, something to fill the breadbasket at dinner, or a sugary nibble to end the meal, continue ahead to mix, knead, and bake your way to emulating the excellence from Dollywood kitchens.

Chocolate Chunk Cookies

Spotlight Bakery, Showstreet

The colossal cookies sold in Showstreet's resident bakery are thick disks of sweet bliss that are ideal for sharing. When baked just right, these cookies have a golden and slightly crunchy outer rim with a decadent chewy center. And if you're tempted to skip chilling the dough...don't do it! Chilling cookie dough before baking allows the butter to solidify, which prevents excessive spreading during baking, resulting in a thick bakery-style cookie.

MAKES 9 COOKIES

½ cup (1 stick) unsalted butter, softened
½ cup packed light brown sugar
¼ cup granulated sugar
1 large egg
¾ teaspoon pure vanilla extract
1⅓ cups all-purpose flour
½ teaspoon baking soda
¼ teaspoon baking powder
½ teaspoon salt
⅓ cup dark chocolate chunks, divided
⅓ cup milk chocolate chunks, divided
⅓ cup semisweet chocolate chips, divided

1. In the bowl of a stand mixer fitted with paddle attachment or in a large bowl using a hand mixer, cream butter with brown sugar and granulated sugar until light and fluffy, about 6 minutes. Add egg and vanilla and mix until combined.
2. In a second medium bowl, stir together flour, baking soda, baking powder, and salt. Add dry ingredients to wet ingredients in three additions, mixing on low until just combined. Reserve 2 tablespoons of each type of chocolate and set aside. Fold in remaining chocolate.
3. Scrape down sides of bowl, cover with plastic wrap, and refrigerate 3 hours or overnight.
4. Preheat oven to 350°F. Line a large baking sheet with parchment paper.
5. Place heaping ¼-cup scoops of dough onto prepared sheet and press down lightly using bottom of each scoop, leaving ample space between each one. Top cookies with reserved chocolate. Return remaining dough to refrigerator.
6. Bake 13 minutes or until cookies are golden brown around the edges. Be careful not to overbake, or cookies will be dry. Let cool on sheet 10 minutes, then use a spatula to transfer to a cooling rack to cool completely. Repeat process with remaining dough, being sure to use a cooled baking sheet.

Butter Crust Bread

Spotlight Bakery, Showstreet

In the park's restaurants, slices of this tender white bread are used as the base for the famous Meatloaf Stackers (see recipe in Chapter 5). Use this bread to build any of your favorite sandwiches, enjoy it spread with softened butter and jam, or use it to make French toast for a decadent breakfast treat.

MAKES 1 LOAF

¾ cup whole milk
¼ cup (½ stick) plus 1 tablespoon unsalted butter, divided
2 teaspoons granulated sugar
1 teaspoon salt
¼ cup warm water (110°F)
1 (¼-ounce) packet active dry yeast
1 large egg, lightly beaten
3¾ cups bread flour, divided

1. To a medium saucepan over medium-low heat, add milk, ¼ cup butter, sugar, and salt. Stir until milk is steaming and sugar is dissolved, about 4 minutes. Remove from heat.
2. In the bowl of a stand mixer, add water and sprinkle yeast on top. Let stand 10 minutes. Add milk mixture to yeast along with egg and 2 cups flour.
3. Use dough hook to mix on low speed until a sticky dough is formed. Add remaining 1¾ cups flour ¼ cup at a time until dough doesn't easily stick to your fingers when touched. You may not use all of the flour.
4. Use dough hook to knead dough 5 minutes, or knead by hand 8 minutes. Press your finger into dough to form a deep dimple. If it fills back in quickly, you've kneaded long enough.
5. Transfer dough to a large lightly oiled bowl and turn over once to coat. Cover bowl with plastic and let rise in a warm place until doubled in size, about 1 hour.
6. Spray an 8" × 4" loaf pan with nonstick cooking spray. Punch down dough and turn out onto a lightly floured surface. Form into loaf and place in prepared pan. Cover with greased plastic wrap and let rise 1 hour. Near end of rise time, preheat oven to 350°F.

7. Bake on center rack up to 50 minutes or until golden. Start checking for doneness after 35 minutes. Tent pan with aluminum foil if top starts to brown too much before bread is done. Bread should sound hollow when tapped on. Use oven mitts to gently tilt bread out of pan to check that it is golden on sides and bottom.
8. Melt remaining 1 tablespoon butter. Remove bread from pan, transfer to a cooling rack, and brush with melted butter.

25-Pound Apple Pie

Spotlight Bakery, Showstreet

It was go big or go home when Dollywood celebrated the park's twenty-fifth anniversary season in 2010 with a colossal apple pie weighing, you guessed it, 25 pounds! The fruity spectacle was baked in a gigantic cast iron skillet holding 20 pounds of sliced and spiced apples tucked into a homemade woven crust. The pie was such a huge hit with park guests during its inaugural season that it ended up sticking around for good and is now a centerpiece of the display case in the bakery. This recipe is scaled down to a more classic-sized pie, though it uses the same techniques as its mammoth namesake.

SERVES 8

For Pie Crust

1 cup (2 sticks) unsalted butter, cold
2½ cups all-purpose flour
1½ teaspoons salt
½ cup cold water

For Apple Pie Filling

5 pounds Granny Smith apples, peeled, cored, and sliced thin
3 tablespoons all-purpose flour
¾ cup granulated sugar
1 cup packed light brown sugar
2 teaspoons ground cinnamon
½ cup (1 stick) unsalted butter, melted
1 large egg, beaten
2 tablespoons coarse turbinado sugar

1. **To make Pie Crust:** Cut butter into small chunks and freeze 15 minutes. In a large bowl, stir together flour and salt. Add butter chunks and use two forks or a pastry blender to cut butter into dry ingredients until mixture resembles coarse crumbs. Drizzle in water and stir until a tacky dough is formed. Using lightly floured hands to combine ingredients will help with this.
2. Turn dough out onto lightly floured surface. Divide into two pieces, one slightly larger than the other, and loosely press each piece into a thick disk. Wrap each disk in plastic wrap and refrigerate 2 hours or up to 3 days.
3. Place an oven rack in lowest position and preheat to 350°F. Grease bottom and sides of a deep-dish 10" cast iron skillet with butter and set aside.
4. Remove dough disks from refrigerator and let sit 5 minutes. Remove plastic from larger disk and roll out onto a floured surface into a 14" round. Place in prepared skillet, press gently around the bottom inside edge, and let excess hang over top edge.
5. Roll out remaining dough disk into a 12" round. Use a round pizza cutter to cut into 1" strips.

continued on next page

6. **To make Apple Pie Filling:** In a separate large mixing bowl, add sliced apples and toss with flour. Add granulated sugar, brown sugar, cinnamon, and melted butter. Use clean hands to mix until apples are evenly coated.
7. Add filling to skillet and press down to pack apples in tightly. The apples will dome up above the edge of the skillet. Place a layer of dough strips horizontally across filling, leaving 1/2" of space between each strip. Fold back every other strip 2/3 of the way across filling. Place one vertical strip down center of filling and unfold folded strips.
8. Fold back horizontal strips that are under vertical strip. Add a second vertical strip next to the first. Unfold folded horizontal strips, then fold back horizontal strips under new vertical strip. Repeat this process until the whole pie is covered with woven crust.
9. Trim excess dough, leaving 1" of overhang. Fold lower crust dough up over the upper dough using a twisting and rolling motion, working around the edges of the entire pie until dough resembles a twisted rope. Brush dough with beaten egg and sprinkle with turbinado sugar.
10. Bake on bottom rack 1 hour and 10 minutes or until apples are tender and filling is hot and bubbly. Insert a fork between the lattice strips to test the apple slices for doneness. Watch pie closely during last 20 minutes. If crust starts to brown too much before apples are done, shield with strips of aluminum foil.
11. Let cool at least 1 hour before slicing and serving.

Scale It Up

To make the full-sized 25-pound pie at home, you will need a 17" cast iron skillet. Multiply crust ingredients by 2 and filling ingredients by 4. Roll out lower crust dough to a 21" round and upper crust dough to a 19" round.

Apple Turnovers

Spotlight Bakery, Showstreet

A "turnover" refers to pastry dough that has been folded in half over a filling and sealed before baking. The Apple Turnovers at Spotlight Bakery are recognized for their use of puff pastry, resulting in a crisp, slightly chewy bite filled with warmly spiced cooked apples. Brushing a beaten egg onto the dough before baking results in a lovely sheen, while a sweet vanilla drizzle adds a hit of extra sweetness and a pretty presentation. For the optimal experience, serve soon after baking while still warm but after the filling has had time to cool to a comfortable temperature.

MAKES 8 TURNOVERS

2 tablespoons unsalted butter
1 teaspoon lemon juice
4 small Granny Smith apples, peeled and sliced
¾ cup packed light brown sugar
1 teaspoon apple pie spice
1 tablespoon cornstarch
2 tablespoons warm water (110°F)
1 (17.3-ounce) box frozen puff pastry, thawed
1 large egg, beaten
1 cup confectioners' sugar
2 tablespoons whole milk
1 teaspoon pure vanilla extract

1. In a medium saucepan over medium heat, melt butter. Stir in lemon juice and add apples, stirring to coat. Cook 3 minutes. Add brown sugar and apple pie spice, stir, and cook 2 minutes more.
2. In a small bowl, whisk cornstarch with water. Add to saucepan, stir, and let simmer 2 minutes or until apples are soft and filling thickens. Remove from heat.
3. Preheat oven to 400°F. Line a large baking sheet with parchment paper and set aside.
4. Gently unfold rectangular pastry sheets and trim to squares. Cut each square into four smaller squares. Discard scraps. Add a generous spoonful of apple filling to center of one square. Fold opposite corners of square together to form a triangle and press edges firmly to seal. Repeat with remaining squares and filling. Place turnovers on prepared sheet, leaving space between each one.
5. Brush turnovers with beaten egg and bake on center rack 13 minutes or until puffed, golden, and shiny. Let cool 15 minutes.
6. In a medium bowl, whisk together confectioners' sugar, milk, and vanilla. If glaze is too thick, add extra milk 1 teaspoon at a time. Drizzle onto cooled turnovers.

Cinnamon Rolls

Spotlight Bakery, Showstreet

The hosts in the kitchen at Spotlight Bakery bake over three hundred of their signature jumbo Cinnamon Rolls every day! A single batch uses 40 pounds of dough that is filled, rolled, and cut into large 5-ounce spirals. After rising, the rolls are baked and coated generously with cream cheese frosting or whatever the seasonal flavor happens to be at the time. These rolls are perfect for a special occasion breakfast. This recipe creates an ample amount of frosting to mimic the thick slathering on Dollywood's rolls, but if you prefer a light spackle, go ahead and cut the frosting ingredients in half.

MAKES 12 ROLLS

For Dough

2 cups warm water (110°F), divided
½ cup plus 1 tablespoon granulated sugar, divided
1 tablespoon active dry yeast
¼ cup (½ stick) unsalted butter, melted
1 teaspoon salt
6 cups all-purpose flour, divided

For Filling

¾ cup (1½ sticks) unsalted butter, softened
1½ cups packed dark brown sugar
2 tablespoons ground cinnamon

1. **To make Dough:** In the bowl of a stand mixer fitted with paddle attachment, stir together ¼ cup water and 1 tablespoon granulated sugar. Sprinkle with yeast and let sit 8 minutes or until foamy and aromatic.
2. Add remaining 1¾ cups water and remaining ½ cup granulated sugar to yeast mixture. Stir. Add melted butter, salt, and 5 cups flour. Mix on low speed until a wet dough is formed. Add remaining 1 cup flour 2 tablespoons at a time until dough is smooth, elastic, and only slightly sticky. You may not use all of the flour, or you may need a bit more.
3. Switch to dough hook attachment and knead on medium-low 6 minutes, or knead by hand 8 minutes. Dough has been kneaded long enough when a dimple made with your finger fills back in quickly.
4. Transfer dough to a large lightly oiled bowl, turn over once to coat, cover with plastic wrap, and let rise in a warm area until doubled in size, about 90 minutes.
5. **To make Filling:** In a medium bowl, mix together softened butter, brown sugar, and cinnamon until a paste is formed. Set aside.

For Frosting

1 cup (2 sticks) unsalted butter, softened
8 ounces (1 block) cream cheese, softened
2 cups confectioners' sugar, sifted
1½ teaspoons pure vanilla extract
¾ teaspoon lemon juice

6. Punch down risen dough and turn out onto floured surface. Roll out into a thin rectangle approximately 25"× 15". Spread filling over dough, covering it right to the edge. Working from the long edge, roll dough tightly into a large log. If thickness varies along the length of the log, gently pull and stretch it until it is even.
7. Line two large baking sheets with parchment paper. Use a sharp serrated knife to cut log into generous 2"-wide pieces and place on prepared sheets, leaving 2" of space between each piece. Lightly cover with greased plastic wrap and let rise in a warm place 1 hour.
8. Near end of rise time, preheat oven to 375°F.
9. Remove plastic wrap and bake on center rack 25 minutes or until rolls are golden brown on top, rotating pans halfway through.
10. **To make Frosting**: In a medium bowl, beat butter with cream cheese until smooth. Add confectioners' sugar in three additions, mixing on low after each, until combined. Add vanilla and lemon juice and mix until smooth. Spread onto warm rolls.

Cheese Danishes

Spotlight Bakery, Showstreet

A sweet treat that originated in Denmark, Danish pastries are made with laminated yeast-leavened dough that yields a tender, flaky, and intensely buttery result. The circular filled pastries seen in many American bakeries are more accurately called "spandauer." And although a cream cheese custard filling is often seen stateside, you won't find that flavor in Denmark, where they opt instead for fruit jams or "remonce," which is butter creamed with sugar and mixed with nuts or spices. You can always find a selection of Danish pastries in Showstreet's Spotlight Bakery. If you're not a cream cheese fan, dollop some fresh fruit jam inside these instead!

SERVES 10

For Danish Dough

1¾ cups all-purpose flour, divided
2 tablespoons granulated sugar
1 teaspoon instant yeast
½ teaspoon salt
1 cup (2 sticks) cold unsalted butter, diced
2 large eggs, divided
7 tablespoons whole milk, divided
1½ teaspoons pure vanilla extract

1. **To make Danish Dough:** In a medium bowl, stir together 1½ cups flour, granulated sugar, yeast, and salt. Use a pastry blender to cut butter into dry ingredients until mixture resembles coarse crumbs.
2. In a small bowl, whisk together 1 egg, 6 tablespoons milk, and vanilla. Add to flour and butter mixture and stir gently to form a dough. If dough is too sticky, add remaining ¼ cup flour 2 tablespoons at a time until dough can be handled with floured hands. You may not use all flour.
3. Shape dough into a rectangle, wrap in plastic wrap, and refrigerate 4 hours.
4. Unwrap dough and place on a lightly floured surface. Roll out a 7" × 15" rectangle. Fold rectangle into thirds. Roll dough out to a large rectangle and fold into thirds. Repeat rolling and folding process a third time, wrap dough in plastic wrap, and refrigerate 1 hour.
5. Repeat previous step once more.

For Filling

8 ounces (1 block) cream cheese, room temperature
1 large egg yolk
1 teaspoon pure vanilla extract
½ teaspoon lemon juice
¼ cup confectioners' sugar

For Drizzle

½ cup confectioners' sugar
2 teaspoons whole milk

6. **To make Filling:** In a medium bowl, use a hand mixer to beat cream cheese, egg yolk, vanilla, and lemon juice. Add confectioners' sugar and mix on low speed until fully combined. Set aside.
7. Line a large rimmed baking sheet with parchment paper. Unwrap dough and roll out a 10" × 15" rectangle on a lightly floured surface. Use a bench scraper or sharp knife to cut into ten pieces roughly equal in size. Place pieces on prepared sheet, leaving space in between each one.
8. Fold all four corners of one piece in toward center and press to make a dent in the middle. Spoon 1⁄10 filling into dent (it is okay if filling overflows slightly). Repeat with remaining dough pieces and filling. Lightly cover with greased plastic wrap and let rise in a warm place 1 hour.
9. Near the end of rise time, preheat oven to 400°F.
10. Prepare an egg wash by whisking remaining 1 egg with remaining 1 tablespoon milk. Remove plastic wrap and brush exposed dough with egg wash. Bake 16 minutes or until golden.
11. **To make Drizzle:** In a small bowl, whisk confectioners' sugar with milk. If mixture is too thick to be drizzled, add more milk ½ teaspoon at a time until correct consistency is reached. Use a spoon to drizzle over warm pastries.

Take a Shortcut

Slash prep time by using frozen puff pastry instead of preparing dough from scratch. Puff pastry is leavened by steam instead of yeast, which will yield a more crispy and airy pastry. Different texture, similar delicious flavor!

Lemon Bars

Spotlight Bakery, Showstreet

Buttery, smooth, and tangy-sweet are appropriate terms to describe the delightful Lemon Bars resting in the glass cases at Spotlight Bakery. To ensure the best citrus flavor at home, use fresh lemons instead of bottled juice. Depending on size, you'll need two to four lemons for these bars. To prevent lemon filling seeping to the bottom of the pan, make sure to add it while the crust is still hot from the oven. For an extra touch, serve each Lemon Bar topped with a thin half-wheel of lemon.

MAKES 24 BARS

For Lemon Filling

1 cup lemon juice
1¼ cups granulated sugar
2 teaspoons cornstarch
6 large eggs
1 large egg yolk

For Shortbread Crust

1 cup (2 sticks) unsalted butter, melted
½ cup granulated sugar
2 teaspoons pure vanilla extract
½ teaspoon salt
1 tablespoon lemon zest
2 cups all-purpose flour
2 tablespoons confectioners' sugar

1. **To make Lemon Filling:** In a medium saucepan over medium heat, stir together lemon juice, sugar, and cornstarch. In a medium mixing bowl, whisk together eggs and egg yolk.
2. Heat lemon juice mixture, stirring occasionally, about 3 minutes or until sugar has completely dissolved. Drizzle ½ cup hot mixture into eggs while whisking constantly, then slowly add egg mixture to saucepan while whisking until fully combined.
3. Continue cooking, stirring frequently, 10 minutes or just until mixture begins to thicken and coats the back of a spoon. Remove from heat immediately. If there are any lumps, press through a fine mesh strainer to remove.
4. **To make Shortbread Crust:** Preheat oven to 325°F.
5. In a separate medium mixing bowl, stir together butter, sugar, vanilla, salt, and lemon zest. Slowly add flour and stir until a thick dough is formed. Press into a glass 9" × 13" baking dish, making sure dough goes all the way to edges of pan and is of even thickness throughout.
6. Bake on center rack 18 minutes or until lightly golden.

continued on next page

7. Pour lemon filling over hot crust and use a nonstick spatula to spread out evenly. Bake an additional 15 minutes or until center is mostly set and jiggles very slightly when pan is shaken.
8. Let cool at room temperature 1 hour, then refrigerate 3 hours.
9. Dust with confectioners' sugar and cut into squares.

Blueberry Muffins

Spotlight Bakery, Showstreet

Did you know Dolly Parton sleeps in her makeup? The star goes to bed all dolled up to be prepared in case of a disaster in the middle of the night that would require her to go outside around other people. If you have your heart set on one of Spotlight Bakery's giant Blueberry Muffins as a late breakfast when the park gates open, sleeping in your makeup might help get you there on time! Or you can try this recipe at home and enjoy a muffin with no care given to what you look like. Serve warm with a smear of butter or a drizzle of honey.

MAKES 6 MUFFINS

½ cup (1 stick) unsalted butter, softened
1 cup granulated sugar
2 large eggs
1½ teaspoons pure vanilla extract
2 cups all-purpose flour
1½ teaspoons baking powder
½ teaspoon baking soda
¼ teaspoon salt
½ cup buttermilk
2 cups fresh blueberries, divided
¼ cup coarse turbinado sugar

1. Preheat oven to 400°F. Line a six-cavity jumbo muffin pan with 6" squares of parchment, letting corners of parchment stick out above edges. Alternatively, butter sides and bottom of cavities.
2. In a large bowl, cream butter and granulated sugar until pale yellow and fluffy, about 6 minutes. Add eggs one at a time, mixing well after each, then add vanilla and mix until combined.
3. In a medium bowl, stir together flour, baking powder, baking soda, and salt. Add half of dry ingredients to wet ingredients along with buttermilk, mixing on low speed 30 seconds. Add remaining dry ingredients and mix on low until a few flour streaks remain.
4. Reserve ⅓ cup blueberries and set aside. Gently fold remaining blueberries into muffin batter, mixing in remaining flour streaks in the process.
5. Distribute batter evenly into prepared muffin pan. Top each muffin with reserved blueberries and turbinado sugar. Bake on center rack 5 minutes, lower oven temperature to 375°F, then bake an additional 20 minutes or until muffins are browned and a toothpick inserted into center of one muffin comes out clean.

Dolly's Banana Pudding

Front Porch Café, Showstreet

Growing up in a poor mountain family, Dolly's mama went to great lengths to keep the bellies of her children full and even managed to provide special treats on occasion. The family's neighbor owned a store and sold them overripe bananas at a discounted price. The bananas were used to create what is still Dolly's favorite dessert to this day: banana pudding. Dollywood's banana pudding is topped with whipped cream, though Dolly herself likes it topped with lightly-baked meringue made with whipped and sweetened egg whites reserved from the separated eggs in the pudding. Whichever way you like it, this simple layered dessert is a real crowd-pleaser.

SERVES 8

¾ cup granulated sugar
¼ cup all-purpose flour
⅛ teaspoon salt
1 large egg
3 large egg yolks
3 cups whole milk
¾ teaspoon pure vanilla extract
3 tablespoons unsalted butter
2½ teaspoons water
¼ teaspoon unflavored gelatin
⅔ cup heavy whipping cream
4 teaspoons confectioners' sugar
20 vanilla wafers, crumbled, plus 8 whole vanilla wafers
4 ripe bananas, peeled and sliced

1. In a heavy-bottomed large saucepan, stir together white sugar, flour, and salt. Add egg and egg yolks and whisk until a paste is formed. Set over medium-low heat and stir in milk, whisking as mixture heats to remove any lumps. Allow to cook, whisking occasionally, about 10 minutes or until mixture thickens. Remove from heat and stir in vanilla and butter. Continue stirring until butter is melted.
2. Let pudding cool 5 minutes, then strain through a fine mesh strainer into a large bowl and cover with plastic wrap, letting wrap touch the top of pudding to prevent a skin from forming. Refrigerate at least 2 hours.
3. In a small microwave-safe bowl, add water and sprinkle gelatin on top. Let sit 3 minutes. Microwave mixture 8 seconds, then stir until gelatin is completely dissolved. Set aside.
4. In a large bowl, add heavy cream. Beat on low speed until cream looks foamy, then stir in confectioners' sugar. Increase speed to medium and continue to beat until cream loosely holds its shape. Drizzle in gelatin

continued on next page

mixture and beat on medium-high speed until soft peaks form. (Lift beaters from cream and turn upside down. If whipped cream on the beater holds its shape but flops over, soft peaks have been achieved.) Beat for an additional 8 seconds, then place bowl in refrigerator while assembling pudding.

5. In eight small Mason jars, create even layers of broken vanilla wafers, pudding, and sliced bananas. Press down on each layer after it is placed. Repeat layers until jars are full. Pipe (using a large open star pastry tip) or spoon whipped cream on top of each jar and decorate with one whole vanilla wafer each.
6. For easier storage of leftovers, layer ingredients in a large glass trifle bowl, spread whipped cream on top, and decorate with whole vanilla wafers. Cover with plastic wrap and refrigerate until ready to serve.

Garlic Cheddar Biscuits

Front Porch Café, Showstreet

Any Southern restaurant worth its salt begins a meal with a basket lined with a gingham napkin and piled high with fluffy, steaming biscuits. Front Porch Café does just that, but it takes the concept one step further with these mouth-wateringly cheesy, garlic-infused biscuits brushed with warm garlic butter and served piping hot. Using a light hand when bringing the dough together is vital to fluffy, tender biscuits.

MAKES 12 BISCUITS

2 cups all-purpose flour
2 teaspoons granulated sugar
1 tablespoon baking powder
2½ teaspoons garlic powder, divided
1 teaspoon salt
2 cups shredded sharp Cheddar cheese
1 cup whole milk
11 tablespoons unsalted butter, melted, divided
1 tablespoon finely chopped fresh parsley

1. Preheat oven to 425°F. Line a large baking sheet with parchment paper and set aside.
2. In a large bowl, stir together flour, sugar, baking powder, 2 teaspoons garlic powder, salt, and cheese. While stirring gently, add milk and 8 tablespoons melted butter. Stir just until dry ingredients are incorporated.
3. Drop scant ¼-cup scoops of dough onto prepared sheet. Bake 11 minutes or until biscuits are golden brown.
4. In a small bowl, combine remaining ½ teaspoon garlic powder, remaining 3 tablespoons melted butter, and parsley. Brush warm biscuits with garlic butter.

Peach Cobbler

Aunt Granny's Restaurant, Rivertown Junction

Peach Cobbler gets its name from the cobbled appearance of the rough and uneven baked dough topping. The origin of the dessert is believed to be an improvisation of peach pie by American settlers who were traveling west and lacked the tools to create a proper pie. Today, Peach Cobbler is the endcap to many Southern meals and takes advantage of the abundance of fresh, juicy peaches during summertime. This recipe can be served warm or cool, and a scoop of vanilla ice cream is always a welcome accompaniment.

SERVES 10

½ cup (1 stick) unsalted butter
1 cup all-purpose flour
⅔ cup granulated sugar, divided
⅔ cup packed light brown sugar, divided
2 teaspoons baking powder
⅛ teaspoon salt
¼ teaspoon ground cinnamon
⅛ teaspoon ground nutmeg
¾ cup whole milk
½ teaspoon pure vanilla extract
5 cups peeled and sliced fresh ripe peaches
1 tablespoon lemon juice
1½ teaspoons cornstarch

1. Preheat oven to 375°F.
2. Cut butter into chunks and add to a 9" × 13" baking dish. Place dish in oven until butter is just melted but has not browned. Watch carefully.
3. In a large mixing bowl, stir together flour, ⅓ cup granulated sugar, ⅓ cup brown sugar, baking powder, salt, cinnamon, and nutmeg. Add milk and vanilla, then stir until just combined. Pour batter over melted butter in prepared baking dish but do not stir.
4. To same mixing bowl, add remaining ⅓ cup granulated sugar, remaining ⅓ cup brown sugar, peaches, and lemon juice. Sprinkle on cornstarch and stir to coat. Pour evenly over batter. Do not stir.
5. Bake on center rack 35 minutes or just until batter is golden and peaches are bubbly. Let cool 20 minutes to allow juices to thicken.

Helpful Tip

Peel peaches easier: Score an X into the skin on two sides of each peach, lower peaches into simmering water for 30 seconds, then immediately transfer to an ice bath. Once peaches have cooled, the skins will slide off.

Grist Mill Cinnamon Bread

Grist Mill, Craftsman's Valley

You know you've arrived at Dollywood's Grist Mill when you see the impressive water wheel powering the mill that grinds 10,000 pounds of grains each season. Look a little farther, and you'll see the line of people—sometimes extending down the sidewalk—waiting for their chance at the warm, buttery cinnamon bread. You can also purchase cinnamon bread from Spotlight Bakery on Showstreet or in Song & Hearth: A Southern Eatery at DreamMore Resort & Spa.

MAKES 2 LOAVES

For Dough

½ cup plus 2 tablespoons warm water (110°F)
1 teaspoon granulated sugar
1 tablespoon unsalted butter, melted
1 teaspoon plus ⅛ teaspoon active dry yeast
1¾ cups bread flour, divided
½ teaspoon salt

For Cinnamon Sugar Topping

6 tablespoons unsalted butter, melted
2 tablespoons ground cinnamon
⅔ cup granulated sugar

For Glaze

1 cup confectioners' sugar
1 tablespoon water
1 tablespoon lemon juice

1. **To make Dough:** Mix warm water, granulated sugar, and melted butter in a small bowl. Sprinkle yeast on top and let sit 6 minutes or until foamy.
2. In the bowl of a stand mixer fitted with paddle attachment, combine 1 cup flour with salt. Add yeast mixture to dry ingredients and mix on medium-low speed to form a sticky dough.
3. Add remaining ¾ cups flour 2 tablespoons at a time, mixing well after each addition. Stop adding flour when Dough feels elastic and does not readily stick to your fingers. You might not use all of the flour, or you may need a tablespoon or two extra.
4. Switch to dough hook attachment and mix on medium-low 6 minutes. Alternatively, knead Dough by hand on a lightly floured surface 8 minutes. Poke Dough with your finger to create a deep dimple. If dimple fills back in quickly, you have kneaded long enough. If not, keep kneading and repeat poke test after another 2 minutes.
5. Place Dough in a large lightly oiled bowl, turn over once to coat, and cover tightly with plastic wrap. Let rise in a warm place 1 hour or until doubled in size.

continued on next page

6. **To make Cinnamon Sugar Topping:** Pour melted butter into a medium-sized container with a wide, flat bottom. In a second medium-sized container with a wide, flat bottom, stir together cinnamon and granulated sugar.
7. Line two 8.5" × 4.5" aluminum loaf pans with parchment paper, letting edges stick out over the top edge of each pan.
8. Punch down Dough and turn out onto a lightly floured surface. Cut into two equal pieces and shape into oval-shaped loaves. Let rise 30 minutes or until Dough has puffed up.
9. Preheat oven to 300°F.
10. Use a sharp knife to make four deep cuts crosswise into each loaf. Handling Dough gently so that you do not deflate it, dip each loaf into melted butter, turning it over once to make sure it is fully coated and butter gets down inside of cuts.
11. Dip loaves into cinnamon sugar mixture, turning each over once to make sure it is fully coated and mixture gets down inside of cuts. Place coated loaves in prepared pans.
12. Bake on center rack 30 minutes or until golden, rotating pans once halfway through. Let cool 5 minutes, then remove bread from pans by lifting up on parchment paper.
13. **To make Glaze:** In a small bowl, whisk together confectioners' sugar with water and lemon juice until smooth. Add water a teaspoon at a time if glaze is too thick. Serve on the side with warm cinnamon bread.

Serving Tip

At the Grist Mill, you can enjoy cinnamon bread one of three ways: plain, with glaze, or with fresh apple butter. Try them all and pick your favorite!

Skillet Cornbread (photo on next page)

Granny Ogle's Ham 'n' Beans, Craftsman's Valley

Cornbread is a fundamental part of Southern meals, and you can find it all over Dollywood and related properties. This recipe is modeled after the Skillet Cornbread at Granny Ogle's Ham 'n' Beans. It is baked in a hot cast iron skillet to yield a crispy crust and with just a slight amount of sugar mixed into the batter to enhance the flavor of the cornmeal without overpowering it. Serve with jam, honey, and butter on the side.

SERVES 8

2 cups self-rising white cornmeal
1 tablespoon granulated sugar
¾ teaspoon salt
4 tablespoons unsalted butter, divided
1 large egg
1½ cups buttermilk

1. Place an 8" cast iron skillet on center rack of oven and preheat to 400°F.
2. In a medium bowl, stir together cornmeal, sugar, and salt.
3. Add 3 tablespoons butter to a small microwave-safe bowl and microwave on high in 20-second increments until melted. Let cool slightly.
4. Add melted butter and egg to batter and stir until mixture resembles coarse crumbs. Slowly add buttermilk while gently stirring, stopping when just combined.
5. Remove hot skillet from oven and add remaining 1 tablespoon butter, moving it around with a spoon until melted. Pour batter into skillet and bake 25 minutes or just until cornbread is golden on top and starts to pull away from edges of skillet.
6. Let cornbread cool in skillet 5 minutes, then carefully turn over onto a large plate.

Did You Know?

In the 1970s, before Dolly Parton came on board and rebranded the park to Dollywood, Granny Ogle's Ham 'n' Beans was known as Big John's Ham & Beans.

Benjamin Bear's Brownies

Sweets and Treats, Wildwood Grove

While visiting the mythical land of Wildwood Grove, you may run into Benjamin Bear's smiling face as he greets and takes photos with guests. The fuzzy black bear can be found either wandering the paths or inside of the Hidden Hollow play area. Just down the path at Sweets and Treats, you'll find Benjamin Bear's Brownies, a bold, fudgy confection served sundae-style that's guaranteed to satisfy any sweet craving. Serve up a batch for a dessert any day of the week or increase the recipe for your next shindig.

SERVES 12

14 tablespoons (1¾ sticks) unsalted butter, cut into small chunks
1⅔ cups semisweet chocolate chips
4 large eggs
1½ cups granulated sugar
2 teaspoons pure vanilla extract
¾ cup all-purpose flour
½ cup cocoa powder
⅛ teaspoon salt
1 cup dark chocolate chips

1. Preheat oven to 350°F. Line a 9" × 13" light metal cake pan with aluminum foil, letting foil come up to the rim of pan. Spray foil with nonstick cooking spray and set aside.
2. Add butter to a large microwave-safe bowl with semisweet chocolate chips. Microwave on high in 30-second increments, stirring after each one, until melted and smooth.
3. In a medium bowl, add eggs, sugar, and vanilla. Whisk until combined. Add to melted chocolate mixture and stir until combined.
4. Add flour, cocoa powder, and salt to bowl. Stir until just combined, then fold in dark chocolate chips. Spread into prepared pan.
5. Bake 40 minutes or until brownies have a shiny crust on top and center is set. Let cool 30 minutes. Lift brownies out of pan by grasping opposite corners of aluminum foil. Cut into squares.

Serving Suggestion

To re-create the park version accurately, serve each brownie topped with a scoop of ice cream, a dollop of whipped cream, and a cherry, then finish with a drizzle of chocolate syrup and a sprinkle of chocolate shavings!

Southern Buttermilk Biscuits

Song & Hearth: A Southern Eatery, Dollywood's DreamMore Resort & Spa

At Dolly's lavish resort, the expansive buffets at onsite restaurant Song & Hearth draw quite the crowd. Tall, hot biscuits are a requisite part of the hearty morning spread. There are a couple of things to keep in mind when making Southern-style biscuits. First, make sure the butter is kept very cold until you are ready to add it to the dough. The little bits of cold butter melt and create steam pockets during the bake, contributing to the rise and softness of the biscuits. Next, use a gentle hand when mixing ingredients and shaping dough, since overworking results in tough, dense biscuits.

MAKES 12 BISCUITS

2 cups all-purpose flour
2 teaspoons baking powder
½ teaspoon baking soda
½ teaspoon salt
6 tablespoons unsalted butter, very cold
1 cup buttermilk
2 tablespoons salted butter, melted

1. Preheat oven to 450°F. Line a large baking sheet with parchment paper and set aside.
2. In a large mixing bowl, stir together flour, baking powder, baking soda, and salt. Cut cold butter into small chunks and add to bowl. Use a pastry blender or two forks to cut butter into dry ingredients until mixture resembles coarse bread crumbs.
3. Make a well in center of bowl and pour in buttermilk. Gently stir until a sticky dough comes together. Turn out onto a well-floured surface. Using floured hands and working gently, fold dough over on itself four times, then use fingertips to press out into a disc 1" thick.
4. Cut biscuits using a 2" round cutter, being sure to press straight down. Do not twist cutter. Place biscuits on prepared sheet, letting sides of biscuits touch each other. Gather scraps of dough and form into a new disc to cut remaining biscuits.
5. Bake on center rack until biscuits are golden on top—start checking for doneness at 12 minutes. Brush hot biscuits with melted butter and serve.

No Buttermilk?

Add 1 tablespoon white vinegar or lemon juice to a measuring cup. Fill with regular milk to make 1 cup and let sit for 5 minutes. Use in place of buttermilk.

Pumpkin Cornbread

Miss Lillian's BBQ Corner, Craftsman's Valley, Harvest Festival

A must-have Southern bread dish paired with harvest flavors of pumpkin and other warm seasonal spices? Talk about the best of both worlds! This thick bread packs substantial flavor and was a Harvest Festival exclusive at Miss Lillian's BBQ Corner, a quick-grab lunch stand situated under the tracks of the Dollywood Express. While you're at it, go ahead and fix a big pot of Three-Bean Pumpkin Chili from Chapter 5 to complete the meal.

SERVES 9

1¾ cups self-rising white cornmeal
¼ cup self-rising flour
⅛ teaspoon salt
½ teaspoon ground cinnamon
½ teaspoon ground ginger
¼ teaspoon ground nutmeg
⅛ teaspoon ground cloves
¼ cup packed light brown sugar
¼ cup (½ stick) unsalted butter, melted and cooled
2 large eggs, lightly beaten
½ cup sour cream
1 cup pumpkin purée

1. Preheat oven to 375°F. Spray bottom and sides of an 8" × 8" light metal baking pan with nonstick cooking spray.
2. In a large mixing bowl, whisk cornmeal, flour, salt, cinnamon, ginger, nutmeg, cloves, and brown sugar.
3. Add melted butter, eggs, and sour cream. Stir until just combined. Fold in pumpkin purée.
4. Transfer batter to prepared pan and bake 30 minutes or until a toothpick inserted into center comes out with a few moist crumbs attached.

Molten Peppermint Chocolate Lava Cakes

Front Porch Café, Showstreet, Dollywood's Smoky Mountain Christmas

Nighttime during Dollywood's Christmas festival is a cozy winterland experience. More than five million lights outline nearly every building, hang from trees, and adorn holiday sculptures. Whether you're enjoying the Christmas festival or tucked in your home, these decadent peppermint lava cakes offer a deliciously warm haven from the outdoor chill. They are a cross between a cake and a soufflé with a molten chocolaty center that flows out onto the plate when cut into with a fork. A scoop of ice cream on the side is a must for this yuletide delight.

SERVES 4

1 tablespoon cocoa powder
½ cup (1 stick) unsalted butter
6 ounces semisweet chocolate, chopped
¼ cup all-purpose flour
¼ cup granulated sugar
⅛ teaspoon salt
2 large eggs
2 large egg yolks
1 teaspoon peppermint extract
4 (½-cup) scoops vanilla ice cream
½ cup crushed peppermint candy

1. Grease four 6-ounce ramekins with butter and dust lightly with cocoa powder. Arrange ramekins on a large baking sheet. Preheat oven to 425°F.
2. In a medium saucepan over medium-low heat, melt butter. Add chocolate, place lid on pan, and remove from heat. Let sit 5 minutes to let chocolate melt, then whisk until smooth.
3. In a small bowl, stir together flour, sugar, and salt. In a second small bowl, whisk eggs with egg yolks. Add flour mixture to melted chocolate and stir to combine. Let cool 5 minutes, then add eggs and peppermint extract. Stir until smooth.
4. Distribute batter evenly into prepared ramekins. Bake 11 minutes or until edges of each cake look done but the tops still look underdone. Let cool 1 minute, then use oven mitts to place a small serving plate upside down onto each ramekin and invert. Gently shake ramekin to help cake release onto plate.
5. Add a scoop of ice cream on top of each cake and sprinkle with peppermint candy.

Change It Up

Omit peppermint extract and peppermint candy to make chocolate lava cakes that are perfect for any time of year!

CHAPTER EIGHT

Country Candy and Ice Cream

No visit to a theme park is complete without splurging on a sweet confection or ice cream treat. You'll find no lack of either in Dollywood, from vintage homemade candy reminiscent of your granny's kitchen, to amusement park favorites like candy apples and a stunning variety of frozen delicacies. Though park gates don't open until midmorning, Dollywood hosts are up bright and early preparing endless batches of classic homemade candies. Sometimes, you can watch the candy craftspeople at the Sweet Shoppe Candy Kitchen as they dip and sprinkle candy apples, slice dense blocks of fudge, and pull colorful taffy. Now you don't need to take a trip to the Smokies (though any excuse is a good excuse...) to sample these goodies. Just browse through this chapter and choose any one of the recipes within—you'll be sugared up in no time!

Showgirl Truffles

Sweet Shoppe Candy Kitchen, Showstreet

If there's one treat in Showstreet's old-fashioned candy shop that is a perfect visual representation of Dolly herself, it is the Showgirl Truffles. The bright-pink chocolate swirls and glittery sprinkles of sugar look just like one of the sparkly outfits that Dolly loves to wear. The truffles are as tasty as they are lovely and are simple to make at home. For the best flavor, choose preserves that are made with real fruit and do not have added sugar or sweeteners.

MAKES 24 TRUFFLES

1 cup heavy cream
16 ounces white chocolate, finely chopped
2 tablespoons raspberry preserves
2 tablespoons strawberry preserves
1 (12-ounce) bag semisweet chocolate chips, divided
1 (12-ounce) bag white candy melts
½ cup pink candy melts
¼ cup coarse sugar

1. In a medium saucepan over medium heat, add cream. Heat until cream begins to steam and a skin starts to form on surface, about 4 minutes. Do not boil. Add white chocolate, remove from heat, and place lid on pan. Let sit 5 minutes, then stir until chocolate is melted.
2. Transfer chocolate to a medium mixing bowl, using a nonstick spatula to scrape pan. Stir in raspberry and strawberry preserves and refrigerate until a solid ganache forms, about 2 hours.
3. Line a large baking sheet with wax paper. Remove bowl from refrigerator. Scoop heaping tablespoons of ganache, roll into balls, and place onto wax paper. Freeze 15 minutes.
4. Reserve ½ cup semisweet chocolate chips and set aside. Place remaining chips in a medium microwave-safe bowl. Microwave on high in 30-second increments, stirring after each one, until chocolate is melted. Place a truffle on top of a fork and lower into melted chocolate, making sure it is fully coated. Return to baking sheet and repeat with remaining truffles. Freeze 15 minutes.

continued on next page

5. Place white candy melts in a microwave-safe bowl and microwave on high in 20-second increments, stirring after each, until melted. Use a fork to lower chocolate-coated truffles into melted white candy until fully coated. Let truffles sit 5 minutes to set, then repeat dipping process—remelting white candy if needed—so that a thick white coating on each truffle is achieved. Let sit until fully hardened, about 1 hour.
6. Place pink candy melts in a sandwich-sized zip-top bag, seal, and microwave on high in 20-second increments, massaging bag after each, until melted. Snip off a tiny corner of bag and pipe looped designs down sides of truffles.
7. Place reserved semisweet chocolate chips in a sandwich-sized zip-top bag, seal, and melt in microwave on high in 20-second increments, massaging bag after each one. Snip off a tiny corner of bag and pipe a small dollop of chocolate onto top of each truffle. Next, pipe looped designs down sides. Sprinkle with coarse sugar and let chocolate harden 1 hour.

Peanut Butter Fudge

Sweet Shoppe Candy Kitchen, Showstreet

Peek inside the glass bakery cases in the Sweet Shoppe Candy Kitchen, and you can't miss the monster-sized hunks of creamy homemade fudge in every flavor you can imagine. Choose from fruity varieties like jelly doughnut, strawberry cheesecake, and orange cream to all-time favorites like classic chocolate, cookies & cream, butter pecan, and visitor favorite—peanut butter! Dollywood sells over two thousand pieces of fudge every single day. For the best robust peanut flavor, choose a no-stir natural peanut butter without added sugar. Be sure to watch the thermometer very carefully to make sure the candy is cooked to the proper temperature.

MAKES 48 PIECES

½ cup (1 stick) unsalted butter
2 pounds (32 ounces) confectioners' sugar
1 (12-ounce) can evaporated milk
1 (7-ounce) jar marshmallow crème
1 (16-ounce) jar creamy peanut butter
1 teaspoon pure vanilla extract

1. Lightly grease bottom and sides of a 9" × 13" baking dish with butter and set aside. Fill a small bowl with cool water and set it next to stove.
2. In a large heavy-bottomed saucepan over medium heat, melt butter. Add confectioners' sugar and evaporated milk. Stir to combine. Attach a candy thermometer to pan, making sure tip is submerged in mixture but is not touching bottom of pan.
3. Cook until mixture reaches soft ball stage and thermometer reads 235°F. Test for doneness by dripping ½ teaspoon of mixture into cool water. If a small ball can be formed under water, it is done. If mixture disintegrates in water, continue cooking for an additional 2 minutes and test again.
4. Remove pan from heat and add marshmallow crème, peanut butter, and vanilla. Stir until mixture is smooth and ingredients are fully combined. Use a nonstick spatula to spread mixture into prepared pan, using spatula to even out top.
5. Let pan sit on counter 3 hours or until fudge is set. Once set, cut into small squares using a sharp knife dipped in hot water.

Chocolate Caramel Apples

Sweet Shoppe Candy Kitchen, Showstreet

Among the tempting displays in Showstreet's homemade candy shop are the trays of candy apples displaying the colors and flavors of the current season. While the apples are a top seller all year, the holiday season can see more than eight hundred apples sold each day! When making your own Dollywood apples, choose crisp, sweet apples such as Honeycrisp, Fuji, or Gala. Change up the toppings however you wish—try different varieties of nuts, colored sprinkles, sanding sugar, swirls of melted candy wafers, or crushed candy and cookies!

SERVES 5

5 crisp, sweet red apples, stems removed, washed, and dried
1 (11-ounce) bag wrapped caramel candies
1 tablespoon water
1 (12-ounce) bag milk chocolate chips
1½ teaspoons canola oil
1½ cups chopped pecans

1. Insert a lollipop stick deep into stem end of each apple. Line a large baking sheet with wax paper lightly sprayed with nonstick cooking spray and set aside.
2. Unwrap caramels and add to a medium saucepan with water. Set over medium-low heat and stir occasionally 12 minutes or until caramels are melted and mixture is smooth. Roll apples in caramel until fully coated, then place upright on prepared sheet. Refrigerate 1 hour.
3. In a large microwave-safe bowl, add chocolate chips and oil. Microwave on high in 25-second increments, stirring after each one, until chocolate has completely melted. Let cool 3 minutes.
4. Dip apples in melted chocolate, letting some caramel remain visible on the top near lollipop stick. Sprinkle immediately with chopped pecans and return to wax paper. Let chocolate stand at room temperature 1 hour or until set and serve.

Chocolate-Covered Frozen Cheesecake

Sweet Shoppe Candy Kitchen, Showstreet

What do you do when you're in a hurry to beat the lines for Wild Eagle but have a jones for something sweet? Cruise through the Sweet Shoppe on your way to the coasters and grab a frozen cheesecake...on a stick! This on-the-go dessert is a surprising underdog of Dollywood treats. The frozen cheesecake softens up as it is eaten, while the snappy chocolate coating keeps everything together. Vary the color of the white chocolate drizzle or add sprinkles while the coating is still wet to match any celebration.

SERVES 10

- 2 cups crushed graham crackers
- 1 cup plus 2 tablespoons granulated sugar, divided
- 10 tablespoons unsalted butter, melted
- 24 ounces (3 blocks) cream cheese, softened
- ½ cup sour cream
- 1 teaspoon pure vanilla extract
- 3 large eggs
- 3 cups semisweet chocolate chips
- 2 teaspoons canola oil
- ⅔ cup white chocolate chips

1. Preheat oven to 350°F. Lightly grease a 9" springform pan with butter. In a medium bowl, stir together graham crackers, 2 tablespoons sugar, and melted butter. Press firmly into bottom of prepared pan.
2. In a large mixing bowl, beat cream cheese, sour cream, remaining 1 cup sugar, and vanilla until light and fluffy. Add eggs one at a time, mixing after each addition, until just combined. Pour into prepared pan.
3. Place a 9" × 13" pan ⅔ full of boiling water on bottom oven rack. Place cheesecake onto center rack and bake until edge is set and center is slightly wobbly. Start checking for doneness after 45 minutes.
4. Run a knife around edge of cake to loosen from pan, cool 1 hour on counter, then refrigerate 6 hours or overnight.
5. Line a large baking sheet with wax paper. Release edge of pan and cut cheesecake into ten equal slices. Arrange slices on prepared sheet. Insert a lollipop stick into curved edge of each slice. Freeze 3 hours.

continued on next page

6. In a large microwave-safe bowl, add semisweet chocolate chips and oil. Microwave on high in 30-second increments, stirring after each one, until melted. Let cool 5 minutes.
7. Working one at a time, hold slice over bowl of melted chocolate. Spoon on a thin layer of chocolate, turning to make sure all sides are coated. Use back of spoon to spread evenly. Return to wax paper. Let sit 5 minutes.
8. In a quart-sized zip-top bag, add white chocolate chips. Microwave on high in 20-second increments, massaging bag after each one, until melted. Let cool 5 minutes. Snip off a tiny corner of bag and drizzle white chocolate over cheesecake slices. Return to freezer 1 hour to set chocolate.

Smoky Mountain Mud

Sweet Shoppe Candy Kitchen, Showstreet

An assortment of treats from Sweet Shoppe Candy Kitchen is a wonderful choice for take-home gifts from the park or as a gift whipped up in your own kitchen! A favorite at the shop, this no-bake "mud" candy is quick, easy, pretty, and delicious. Dollywood makes dark, milk, and white chocolate versions of Smoky Mountain Mud, and you can do the same by varying the type of chocolate chips used.

MAKES 60 CANDIES

2 pounds (32 ounces) milk chocolate chips
2 cups creamy peanut butter
2 cups mini marshmallows
2 cups Rice Krispies cereal
1 cup dry-roasted peanuts
¾ cup white chocolate chips

1. In a large microwave-safe bowl, add milk chocolate chips. Microwave on high in 30-second increments, stirring after each one, until melted. Stir in peanut butter, then fold in marshmallows, cereal, and peanuts.
2. Spoon sixty 2"-diameter candies onto wax paper. Let cool 90 minutes.
3. Add white chocolate chips to a quart-sized zip-top bag and seal. Microwave on high in 25-second increments, massaging bag after each one, until melted. Snip off a tiny corner of bag and drizzle melted chocolate over candies. Let cool an additional 90 minutes or until set.

Homemade Taffy

Sweet Shoppe Candy Kitchen, Showstreet

Bins of colorful homemade taffy create a rainbow of sugar in the park's candy kitchen. Any flavors you can dream up are cooked, pulled, and cut right on site, from classics like strawberry, vanilla, and chocolate to more creative tastes like root beer, buttered popcorn, and maple bacon. Dollywood's candy-making hosts cook their taffy to a precise 249 degrees Fahrenheit to achieve the ideal texture—not too soft and not too hard. Use this recipe as a base for making any flavor of taffy. Super-strength flavoring oils known as "candy oils" are recommended for best results, and you can use any flavor and coordinating food coloring that you want.

MAKES 70 PIECES

2 cups granulated sugar
1⅓ cups light corn syrup
2 tablespoons unsalted butter
1 teaspoon unflavored gelatin
1 cup water
1 teaspoon candy oil flavoring, any variety
4 drops food coloring, any color

1. Add sugar, corn syrup, and butter to a large heavy-bottomed pot fitted with a candy thermometer. Set over medium heat. In a small bowl, stir together gelatin with water.
2. Stir corn syrup mixture 3 minutes or until sugar dissolves. Continue heating, without stirring, until thermometer reads 249°F. Watch temperature closely. Stir in gelatin mixture and flavoring. Remove from heat. Stir in food coloring.
3. Transfer to a lightly buttered medium-sized heat-resistant bowl and let cool until able to be handled. Hold taffy in both hands and stretch out to about 15" long. Fold taffy over on itself and repeat stretching and folding until taffy is much lighter in color and is more difficult to pull, about 12 minutes.
4. Shape taffy into a log approximately 30" long and 1" thick. Use kitchen shears to snip into seventy individual candies. Wrap each candy in a small square of wax paper and twist ends together to seal.

Waffle Bowl Sundaes

Showstreet Ice Cream, Showstreet

This treat marries the best kind of ice cream cone to a hot fudge sundae. You've got plenty of room to pile on multiple scoops of ice cream and toppings in a delicious bowl-shaped waffle cone. Showstreet Ice Cream scoops Mayfield ice cream into their triple-scoop waffle bowl sundaes and offers tempting combinations such as Hershey's Hot Fudge and Oreo Sundae. When making homemade waffle bowls, be sure not to overcook them before shaping, as they will become brittle and break easily. Don't forget to add all of your favorite sundae toppings like hot fudge, caramel sauce, chopped nuts, fun sprinkles, whipped cream, and a bright-red cherry to top the whole thing off!

SERVES 4

1 large egg
¼ cup granulated sugar
¼ teaspoon pure vanilla extract
⅓ cup all-purpose flour
3 tablespoons whole milk
2 tablespoons salted butter, melted and cooled
12 (½ cup) scoops ice cream, any flavors

1. Preheat waffle cone maker. Arrange four 6-ounce ramekins upside down on a piece of wax paper, leaving space between each one. Spray ramekins lightly with cooking spray. You can also use an inverted jumbo muffin pan.
2. In a medium bowl, whisk egg with sugar and vanilla until smooth. Add flour and milk, stir gently, then add melted butter and stir until just combined.
3. Pour ¼ cup batter into center of hot waffle cone maker and close lid tightly. Cook until lightly golden, 1–2 minutes. Use a spatula to lay hot waffle over a ramekin and gently form it into an upside-down bowl shape. Repeat with remaining batter. Let cool 15 minutes or until hardened.
4. Fill bowls with 3 scoops ice cream each and serve.

No Waffle Cone Maker?

Preheat oven to 325°F and line a large baking sheet with parchment paper. Create thin circles using ¼ cup of batter at a time. Bake for 10 minutes or until lightly golden, then immediately transfer to prepared ramekins and let cool to harden.

Chocolate-Dipped Frozen Bananas

Splash & Dash Sundries, Dollywood's Splash Country

This popular amusement park frozen treat can be traced all the way back to 1940 with the first frozen banana stand, The Original Frozen Banana, in Orange County, California. This delightful alternative to an ice cream cone gained a massive following and can be found all over the place now, including in both Dollywood parks! While the bananas are kept whole in Dollywood, this recipe cuts them in half for a better texture when freezing at home. Change up the toppings by replacing the chopped peanuts with an equivalent amount of colorful sprinkles, shredded coconut, or crushed chocolate sandwich cookies.

SERVES 6

3 large firm yellow bananas, peeled and halved crosswise
8 ounces semisweet chocolate chips
1 tablespoon canola oil
⅔ cup finely chopped peanuts

1. Insert a Popsicle stick into each banana half and place on a medium baking sheet lined with wax paper. Freeze 30 minutes.
2. While bananas are in freezer, place chocolate chips and oil in a medium microwave-safe bowl with a bottom wide enough to accommodate one banana half. Microwave on high in 30-second increments, stirring after each one, until melted.
3. Remove bananas from freezer, roll in chocolate, and immediately sprinkle with chopped peanuts. Freeze 1 hour and serve.

Berries 'n Cream

Berries N Cream, Dollywood's Splash Country

Berries N Cream is your go-to ice cream shop when visiting the water park on a hot summer day. On the menu is hand-scooped ice cream, soft serve, waffle bowls, and ice cream floats. The shop's namesake treat, Berries 'n Cream, is served layered with soft serve ice cream and a sweet fruit sauce. It's difficult to make true soft serve at home without specialized equipment, but this trick of folding sweetened whipped cream into softened ice cream is a close substitute.

SERVES 4

3 cups vanilla ice cream
¼ cup heavy whipping cream
4 tablespoons granulated sugar, divided
½ teaspoon pure vanilla extract
¼ cup water
2 teaspoons cornstarch
1 pound fresh strawberries, hulled and finely chopped
1 teaspoon lemon juice

1. Place a large metal mixing bowl and beaters for hand mixer in freezer 1 hour.
2. Place ice cream on counter to soften while completing next steps. Add whipping cream to chilled bowl and whip on medium-high speed until soft peaks form. Add 1 tablespoon sugar and vanilla and mix until just combined. Fold in softened ice cream and transfer to a gallon-sized zip-top freezer bag. Freeze 2 hours or until firm but not solid.
3. In a medium saucepan over medium heat, add water and cornstarch. Whisk until cornstarch is dissolved. Add strawberries, remaining 3 tablespoons sugar, and lemon juice. Cook until mixture starts to bubble, stirring occasionally, about 5 minutes. Remove from heat and let cool 20 minutes or until room temperature.
4. Remove soft serve from freezer and cut off one corner of bag. Pipe a layer of soft serve into four large Mason jars. Spoon in a generous layer of strawberry sauce, then pipe in another layer of soft serve. Top with another spoonful of sauce and serve.

Liege Waffle Ice Cream Sandwiches

Showstreet Ice Cream, Showstreet, Dollywood's Flower & Food Festival

A Liege waffle is different from a Belgian waffle in a few distinct ways. Instead of batter ladled into a waffle iron to fill the cavities, Liege waffles are made from a thicker bread-like dough that is formed by hand and placed onto the iron. Pearl sugar—small pieces of compacted sugar—is mixed into the dough by hand. The sugar doesn't fully dissolve when the waffles are cooked, resulting in little pockets of sweetness throughout. During the Flower & Food Festival, Liege waffles are dipped into melted chocolate, sprinkled with pistachio nuts, and sandwiched with the ice cream flavor of your choosing. Create any combination you want!

SERVES 5

¾ cup warm whole milk (110°F)
1 (¼-ounce) packet active dry yeast
1 teaspoon granulated sugar
12 tablespoons (1½ sticks) unsalted butter, melted
2 large eggs
3½ cups all-purpose flour
½ teaspoon salt
1 teaspoon pure vanilla extract
1⅓ cups Belgian pearl sugar
8 ounces semisweet chocolate chips
1 teaspoon canola oil
⅔ cup chopped pistachios
5 (½ cup) scoops ice cream, any flavor

1. In a medium bowl, add warm milk and sprinkle yeast and granulated sugar on top. Let sit 8 minutes or until foamy and fragrant. Add melted butter and eggs. Whisk to combine.
2. In a large bowl, stir together flour and salt. Add yeast mixture and vanilla to dry ingredients and mix on low speed 3 minutes. Transfer dough to a separate large lightly oiled bowl, turn once to coat, cover with plastic wrap, and let rise in a warm place 40 minutes.
3. Preheat Belgian waffle iron. Set a large piece of wax paper on countertop. Fold pearl sugar into dough by hand and divide into ten equal balls.
4. Spray waffle iron generously with nonstick cooking spray. Add a dough ball to center of waffle iron, close lid, and cook until golden and crispy. Cook times will vary depending on waffle iron—check after 3 minutes. Carefully transfer finished waffle to wax paper and repeat with remaining dough.

5. In a microwave-safe bowl, add chocolate chips and oil. Microwave on high in 25-second increments, stirring after each one, until chocolate is melted. Dip one end of each waffle into chocolate, place on wax paper, and sprinkle immediately with chopped pistachio nuts.
6. Scoop ice cream onto five waffles and top with remaining five waffles. Serve immediately.

Fruit Paletas

Seasonal Culinary Booth, Dollywood's Flower & Food Festival

Paletas are Mexican-style creamy ice pops made with fresh fruit. They are a seasonal frozen treat sold during the springtime Flower & Food Festival. Spring days in East Tennessee can start with crisp mornings that quickly soar to temperatures in the 80s by the afternoon, so a frozen treat can be your best friend while meandering around and enjoying the colorful blooms. Change up the flavors using different fruit purées such as pineapple, mango, or fresh watermelon!

SERVES 12

- 1 pound fresh strawberries, hulled
- 1 pound ripe peaches, peeled and pits removed
- 2 tablespoons cold water, divided
- 1 (14-ounce) can sweetened condensed milk, divided
- 1 cup whole milk, divided

1. Place strawberries in a food processor and pulse until smooth. Transfer purée to a medium bowl. Rinse food processor and repeat step with peaches. Transfer peach purée to a second medium bowl.
2. Place 1 tablespoon water, half can of condensed milk, and ½ cup whole milk in bowl with strawberry purée. Repeat with peach purée. Stir to combine.
3. Transfer fruit mixtures to Popsicle molds and insert a Popsicle stick into each one. Freeze 6 hours or until solid.

Celebration Sundaes (photo on next spread)

Sweets and Treats, Wildwood Grove, Smoky Mountain Summer Celebration

Dollywood's summer festival is all about colors and fanfare, and as far as festival treats go, the Celebration Sundae sold in Wildwood Grove is undeniably the most fun. The dessert, served with an upside-down waffle cone that showers the ice cream in colorful sprinkles and candies when removed, comes with a fresh and crispy chocolate-covered churro doughnut. This recipe will make a full batch of doughnuts, so you can scale up the sundae ingredients to create as many as you need, or keep the extra doughnuts around to have with coffee the next morning—yum!

SERVES 2

For Churro Doughnuts

½ cup plus 1 tablespoon granulated sugar, divided
1 teaspoon ground cinnamon
1 cup water
¼ cup (½ stick) unsalted butter, diced
¼ teaspoon salt
1 cup all-purpose flour
1 large egg
1 teaspoon pure vanilla extract
1 quart canola oil (for fry method)
2 tablespoons unsalted butter, melted (for oven method)
¾ cup heavy cream
1 cup semisweet chocolate chips

1. **To make Churro Doughnuts:** In a small bowl, stir together ½ cup sugar with cinnamon and set aside.
2. In a medium saucepan, combine remaining 1 tablespoon sugar with water, diced butter, and salt. Set over medium-high heat and bring to a low boil.
3. Once boiling, reduce heat to low and stir in flour until a smooth dough is formed. Remove from heat and let cool 10 minutes. Line a large baking sheet with parchment paper.
4. Add egg and vanilla to dough and use a hand mixer to blend until completely smooth. Fit a large piping bag with a ½" closed star tip and fill with dough. Pipe nine doughnut shapes onto prepared sheet. Freeze 30 minutes.
5. **Fry Method:** In a wide sauté pan fitted with a thermometer, add oil 1½" deep and set over medium heat. Heat oil to 375°F. Working in batches, fry doughnuts 4 minutes or until deep golden, turning halfway through. Don't crowd pan, or doughnuts will stick together. Transfer to a large plate lined with paper towels, drain 10 seconds, then sprinkle with cinnamon sugar mixture.

continued on next page

For Sundaes

4 (½ cup) scoops vanilla ice cream
¼ cup caramel ice cream syrup
2 large waffle cones
⅔ cup M&M's candies
¼ cup chocolate sprinkles
¼ cup red, white, and blue sprinkles

6. **Oven Method:** Preheat oven to 350°F. Remove baking sheet from freezer and bake on center rack 20 minutes, then turn oven to broil on high and broil until golden, checking every 2 minutes. Brush doughnuts with melted butter and coat with cinnamon sugar mixture.
7. In a small saucepan over medium-low heat, add cream and heat to steaming. Remove from heat, add chocolate chips, and place lid on pan. Let sit 5 minutes to melt chocolate, then whisk until smooth. Dip one side of each doughnut into warm chocolate and return to the same prepared sheet to let chocolate set, about 30 minutes.
8. **To make Sundaes:** Scoop ice cream into two sundae bowls. Drizzle with caramel syrup. In waffle cones, distribute M&M's candies; chocolate sprinkles; and red, white, and blue sprinkles. Working quickly, turn waffle cone upside down over ice cream and press down, trapping the sprinkles and candy inside. Place a doughnut in each bowl and serve.

Take a Shortcut

Turn this into a quick treat by using store-bought doughnuts. Buy cinnamon sugar doughnuts and dip into melted chocolate for a close replacement—or use any flavor you want!

Brown Butter Rice Krispy Treats

Spotlight Bakery, Showstreet, Harvest Festival

The Spotlight Bakery, located not far from Dollywood's main entrance, is the place to be during the Harvest Festival. The aroma of pumpkin, apple, and warmly spiced treats is overwhelming as you take in the glorious harvest colors of red, yellow, and orange. Cereal treats are available throughout the season, but this recipe adds some extra flair by first cooking butter until golden, releasing a nutty caramel flavor. Make fall-themed treats or match any holiday or occasion you want by changing up the colors of the candy melts and sprinkles.

MAKES 12 TREATS

- ¾ cup (1½ sticks) unsalted butter
- 1 tablespoon packed light brown sugar
- 2 (10-ounce) bags mini marshmallows
- 1 teaspoon pure vanilla extract
- 10 cups Rice Krispies cereal
- ¾ cup orange candy melts
- ½ cup colorful sprinkles

1. Spray a 9" × 13" pan with nonstick cooking spray and set aside.
2. In a large heavy-bottomed pot over medium heat, melt butter. Let butter simmer while stirring frequently until it turns a rich golden color, about 9 minutes. Watch it carefully to prevent burning.
3. Add brown sugar to pot and stir to dissolve. Add marshmallows and stir constantly 3 minutes or just until marshmallows are melted and mixture is completely smooth. Remove from heat.
4. Stir in vanilla. Add cereal and use a nonstick spatula to fold it in until fully coated. Immediately transfer to prepared pan and lightly press down. Don't press too hard, or treats will be dense. Let cool 1 hour, then cut into squares.
5. In a small microwave-safe bowl, add candy melts and microwave on high in 20-second increments, stirring after each one, until melted. Dip one end of treats in melted candy and decorate with sprinkles.

CHAPTER NINE

Back Porch Sips

If there's one thing that can be counted on during the summer months in East Tennessee, it's the heat! Whether you enjoy strolling through the charming paths of Dollywood on a blistering day, relaxing in a rocking chair on the back porch on a sunny August afternoon, or sipping a summer favorite in the cooler months, you'll find this chapter to be a party of creative iced beverages, fruity frozen slushies, flavored teas, and creamy milkshakes. And if something a little stronger is more your vibe, you'll learn how to make the bestselling cocktails from DreamMore Resort & Spa's creative bar specialists. Of course, this collection would be utterly incomplete without a recipe for perfectly sweet iced tea, the drink staple of the South!

Frozen Strawberry Lemonade

Showstreet Frozen Lemonade, Showstreet

When the sun is high and the temperature is steamy, cooling off with a frosty, fruity beverage is the perfect remedy. At Showstreet Frozen Lemonade, you can find many flavors of this treat, such as plain lemonade, strawberry, blue raspberry, lemon-lime, and cherry. Vary the thickness of this beverage by drizzling in a little extra lemonade after blending to thin. And the next time you are in Dollywood, pick up a refillable souvenir mug to beat the heat all day long!

SERVES 2

- 1 cup Minute Maid lemonade
- 2 cups frozen strawberries
- 1 tablespoon granulated sugar

To the pitcher of a high-powered blender, add lemonade, strawberries, and sugar. Blend on high until completely smooth. Pour into two glasses and serve.

Sweet Tea

Front Porch Café, Showstreet

It is a little-known fact that Sweet Tea gained popularity in the South during the years of Prohibition. Fancy glassware wasn't getting much use anymore, and Southerners were desperate for tasty, comforting beverages to replace their favorite alcoholic drinks. The sweetened beverage really marked its territory toward the end of the 1920s when it began showing up in Southern cookbooks. While Front Porch Café and its homey vibe is an ideal place to sip on some Sweet Tea, you can find it at any of the full-service restaurants in the park. At home, try it straight up or add a squeeze of lemon or a sprig of fresh mint for extra refreshment.

SERVES 6

1⁄16 teaspoon baking soda
2 cups boiling water
6 bags black tea
¾ cup granulated sugar
6 cups cold water

1. Place baking soda in a heat-resistant pitcher that has a capacity of more than 64 ounces. Add boiling water and tea bags. Cover pitcher and steep 15 minutes.
2. Remove tea bags, add sugar, and stir until sugar is completely dissolved.
3. Pour in cold water, stir, and let sit at room temperature 1 hour. Then refrigerate 4 hours or until chilled. Serve in glasses filled with ice.

Cut the Sugar

Leave sugar out to make unsweet iced tea and, when serving, stir in any of your favorite sugar substitutes instead.

Orange Cream Milkshake

Red's Drive-In, Jukebox Junction

Stepping into Red's is like being propelled back in time to the 1950s, so much so that you almost expect the patrons to be wearing poodle skirts and letterman jackets with greased-back hair and high ponytails. No detail is overlooked, from the shiny red booths and chrome accents to the retro napkin holders and classic jukebox. In addition to standard diner fare like burgers and hot dogs, the standout treat at Red's is their thick and creamy milkshakes. The restaurant is forever coming out with creative new flavors, including this creamy citrus delight reminiscent of Creamsicle ice cream bars.

SERVES 1

½ cup (heaping) vanilla ice cream
½ cup (heaping) orange sherbet
¼ cup whole milk
⅛ teaspoon pure orange extract
⅓ cup whipped cream
1 orange slice

1. In a high-powered blender, add ice cream, sherbet, milk, and orange extract. Blend just until smooth. If too thick, drizzle in extra milk 2 teaspoons at a time.
2. Pour into a tall glass, top with whipped cream, and garnish with orange slice.

Honey Sage Lemon Drop

Song & Hearth: A Southern Eatery, Dollywood's DreamMore Resort & Spa

Flipping through the robust cocktail menu at Song & Hearth can be overwhelming when trying to decide which of the tasty tipples to try. But the talented mixologists promise you won't be disappointed with the bestselling Honey Sage Lemon Drop, a vodka-based shaken mixture of muddled sage leaves with notes of citrus and honey. The sage leaves are grown right outside of the bar in the resort's own herb garden maintained by DreamMore chefs. This is a simple cocktail that takes only a few minutes to re-create at home so that you're never too far away from enjoying a sip of Dollywood.

SERVES 1

1 tablespoon granulated sugar
4 fresh sage leaves, divided
1 ounce honey syrup
2 ounces vodka
1 ounce triple sec
2 tablespoons lemon juice

1. Sprinkle sugar onto a small saucer. Wet the rim of a martini glass with water and roll in sugar.
2. Add 2 sage leaves and honey syrup to a cocktail shaker and muddle gently. Fill with ice and add vodka, triple sec, and lemon juice. Shake vigorously.
3. Strain into prepared martini glass. Garnish with remaining 2 sage leaves.

Mocktail Version

Make this cocktail nonalcoholic by replacing the vodka and triple sec with 3 ounces of nonalcoholic citrus spirits.

Bourbon Peach Smash

Song & Hearth: A Southern Eatery, Dollywood's DreamMore Resort & Spa

Visitors to Song & Hearth at Dollywood's immense resort are met with a comfortable vibe of rustic glam. Just outside of the main dining room is the Lounge, which boasts a full-service bar accented by an impressive Mason jar mural. It is here, under the reclaimed barn wood ceiling, where mixology magic happens. The bar boasts a multipage menu of signature cocktails, and this Bourbon Peach Smash is a patron favorite. A juicy, ripe peach will yield the best fresh fruit flavor, though if peaches are not currently in season, you can use 2 tablespoons of peach preserves instead.

SERVES 1

½ small ripe peach, diced
6 fresh mint leaves, divided
1 tablespoon amber honey
½ cup crushed ice
1½ ounces bourbon
4 ounces ginger ale, chilled
1 lemon slice

1. Add peach, 4 mint leaves, and honey to a rocks glass. Muddle gently.
2. Fill glass ¾ full with ice. Add bourbon, top off glass with ginger ale, and stir gently.
3. Garnish glass with remaining 2 mint leaves and lemon slice.

Mocktail Version

Make this cocktail nonalcoholic by replacing the bourbon with ½ ounce of lemon juice and 1 ounce of peach juice.

Apricot Cherry Green Tea

Seasonal Culinary Booth, Festival of Nations

The Festival of Nations was an event that exhibited traditional music and dance performances from around the world as well as international cuisine, such as this unique beverage served at the South Korea booth. Serve a cold glass with Beef Bulgogi Nachos (see recipe in Chapter 4).

SERVES 6

5 bags green tea
3 cups boiling water
2 tablespoons granulated sugar
2 (11.3-ounce) cans apricot nectar, chilled
1 cup cold water
¼ cup cherry syrup
6 fresh cherries
6 fresh apricot slices

1. Place tea bags in a large heat-resistant pitcher and add boiling water. Cover pitcher and steep 12 minutes. Remove tea bags and discard.
2. Stir in sugar until completely dissolved. Pour in apricot nectar, cold water, and cherry syrup. Stir well. Let sit at room temperature 1 hour, then refrigerate 4 hours or until chilled.
3. Serve in tall glasses filled with ice, garnished with cherries and apricot slices.

Shillelagh

Seasonal Culinary Booth, Festival of Nations

A shillelagh is an Irish walking stick that has become a symbol of the Irish way of life, and the traditional Shillelagh cocktail is a strong and fruity concoction. Because no alcohol is sold in Dollywood, the festival version of this drink is fruit-forward with fresh peach juice in place of liquor.

SERVES 1

½ cup ice cubes
1 teaspoon lemon juice
4 ounces peach juice
1 teaspoon confectioners' sugar
3 fresh raspberries
1 slice lemon

1. Add ice to a cocktail shaker, then pour in lemon juice, peach juice, and confectioners' sugar. Shake and strain into a rocks glass filled with ice.
2. Drop in fresh raspberries and garnish edge of glass with lemon slice.

Pink Watermelon Lemonade Slushies

Seasonal Culinary Booth, Dollywood's Flower & Food Festival

While frozen lemonade is sold in the park all season long, the Flower & Food Festival adds a refreshing twist to this favorite frosty treat: watermelon! Enjoy a glass while taking in the aroma of fresh flowers at the festival or simply relaxing in your own backyard.

SERVES 2

4 cups cubed frozen seedless watermelon
2 cups lemonade, chilled
2 tablespoons grenadine syrup
2 small wedges fresh watermelon
2 slices lemon

1. Combine frozen watermelon, lemonade, and grenadine in a high-powered blender and blend until completely smooth. If slushie is too thick, drizzle in extra lemonade 2 tablespoons at a time and blend. Repeat as needed until slushie can easily be sipped through a straw.
2. Pour into medium-sized glasses and garnish each glass with a fresh watermelon wedge and lemon slice.

Butterflies!

Always striving to create immersive experiences in the park, Dollywood added an interactive digital exhibit to the springtime festival called Dolly's Butterfly Garden. Guests can walk through a special area in the Chasing Rainbows museum while digitized butterflies float about, coming and going based on movement.

Strawberry Hibiscus Fresca

Seasonal Culinary Booth, Dollywood's Flower & Food Festival

In addition to looking pretty, hibiscus flowers have many applications in the kitchen and are used in tea, chilled beverages, jam, and salads. Hibiscus blooms have a lovely tart flavor, and the flowers can be eaten safely right off the plant! Dollywood created a thirst-quenching combination of a cold strawberry hibiscus fresca topped with a smooth and sweet cold foam for their springtime festival. The drink is finished with a fresh strawberry and a sprinkling of hibiscus flowers that you can actually eat!

SERVES 4

4 cups water
4 bags hibiscus tea
6 tablespoons granulated sugar
2 cups chopped fresh strawberries, hulled
⅔ cup heavy cream
1 cup whole milk
4 tablespoons vanilla syrup
4 fresh whole strawberries
4 tablespoons fresh hibiscus flower petals

1. In a small saucepan, bring water to a boil on medium-high heat. Once boiling, remove from heat, add tea bags, and steep for 10 minutes. Stir in sugar until dissolved.
2. Purée chopped strawberries in a blender and press through a fine mesh strainer into a small heat-resistant pitcher. Top with tea and stir. Add more sugar if desired. Let stand at room temperature 1 hour, then chill in refrigerator 4 hours or until cold.
3. In a large, deep bowl, stir together cream, milk, and vanilla syrup. Using a hand mixer on medium-high speed, beat for 2 minutes or until frothy, then beat on high for an additional minute or until the mixture thickens and is foamy.
4. Pour fresca into four medium-sized glasses filled with ice, leaving at least 1" of space on top. Spoon a layer of sweet cold foam on top and garnish each glass with 1 whole strawberry and 1 tablespoon hibiscus flowers.

Blue Woog

Market Square BIG SKILLET®, Rivertown Junction, Dollywood's Flower & Food Festival

This bright-blue beverage, accented with a sunny yellow pineapple wedge, was a brand-new addition to the 2022 Flower & Food Festival. A citrus-forward drink, it uses nonalcoholic blue curaçao syrup to add beautiful color, a pleasant slight bitterness, and a nip of orange flavor. Guests who want to experience this and other festival food options can purchase a tasting pass, which allows purchase of up to five menu items for a lower price than buying the items separately.

SERVES 1

2 ounces pineapple juice
1 ounce lemon juice
1 ounce blue curaçao syrup
4 ounces lemonade
4 ounces lemon-lime soda
1 small pineapple wedge

Fill a tall glass halfway with cubed ice. Add pineapple juice, lemon juice, blue curaçao, and lemonade. Stir. Top with lemon-lime soda and garnish with pineapple wedge.

Santa's Chilled Cocoa

Market Square BIG SKILLET®, Rivertown Junction, Dollywood's Smoky Mountain Christmas

The hosts at Market Square serve up this beautiful holiday sipper during the Christmas festival, and it's almost too cute to drink! Served in a clear cup to show off the sweet cream and peppermint-kissed chilled cocoa layers, the presentation is finished with a sprinkle of cocoa powder and shaved chocolate. For the best flavor, choose a good-quality hot cocoa mix with a rich chocolate flavor. If you aren't a fan of the combination of chocolate and peppermint, simply leave out the extract!

SERVES 2

1½ cups warm whole milk (110°F)
2 (1.38-ounce) envelopes hot cocoa mix
¼ teaspoon peppermint extract
⅔ cup heavy cream
1 cup cold whole milk
4 tablespoons vanilla syrup
⅔ cup ice cubes
1 teaspoon cocoa powder
2 tablespoons chocolate shavings

1. Add warm milk, hot cocoa mix, and peppermint extract to a large heat-resistant jar. There should be a few inches of room left at the top. Place lid on jar and shake until mix dissolves. Refrigerate 45 minutes.
2. In a large, deep bowl, stir together cream, cold milk, and vanilla syrup. Use a hand mixer on medium-high speed to beat for 3 minutes or until frothy, then beat on high for an additional minute or until the mixture thickens and is foamy.
3. Remove cocoa from refrigerator and add ice to jar. Replace lid and shake vigorously for 1 minute.
4. To two tall glasses, spoon a layer of sweet foam, then distribute chilled cocoa and ice evenly between glasses. Top with a thick layer of foam and garnish with cocoa powder and chocolate shavings.

Appendix

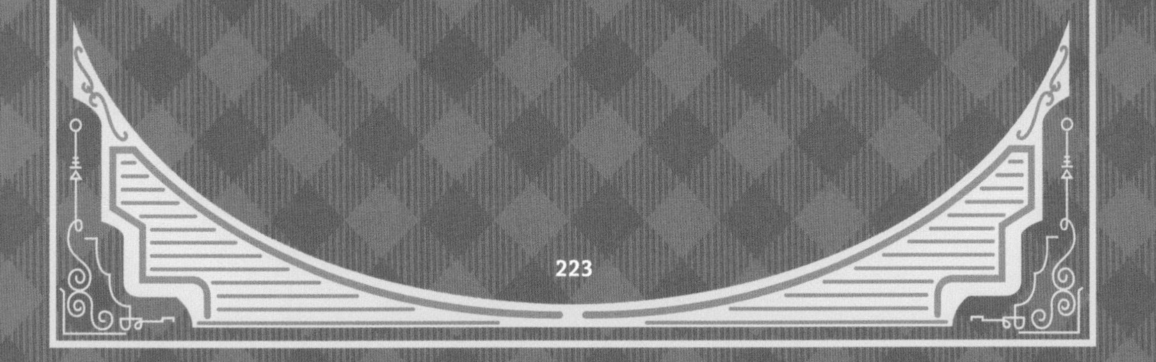

Dollywood Park Maps

Use the following maps and festival key to discover where you can find each of the recipes in Part 2 within Dollywood! The first map shows all four Dollywood locations: Dollywood (the main park), Dolly Parton's Stampede Dinner Attraction, Dollywood's Splash Country, and Dollywood's DreamMore Resort & Spa. The second map shows the eleven areas of the main park: Adventures in Imagination, Showstreet, Rivertown Junction, Jukebox Junction, Country Fair, The Village, Owens Farm, Craftsman's Valley, Wilderness Pass, Wildwood Grove, and Timber Canyon. Each map includes a numbered key so you can match a location on the map to what dishes and/or drinks are found there, as well as the corresponding chapter of this book where each recipe in that location can be found.

Dollywood Festivals

Since the festivals at Dollywood are not permanent fixtures, their locations will not be found on either map. Recipes for these special events are listed here.

Festival of Nations

Dollywood's Flower & Food Festival

Smoky Mountain Summer Celebration

Harvest Festival

Dollywood's Smoky Mountain Christmas

Dollywood Properties

(shown at right)

1 Dolly Parton's Stampede Dinner Attraction

2 Dollywood's Splash Country

3 Dollywood's DreamMore Resort & Spa, Song & Hearth: A Southern Eatery

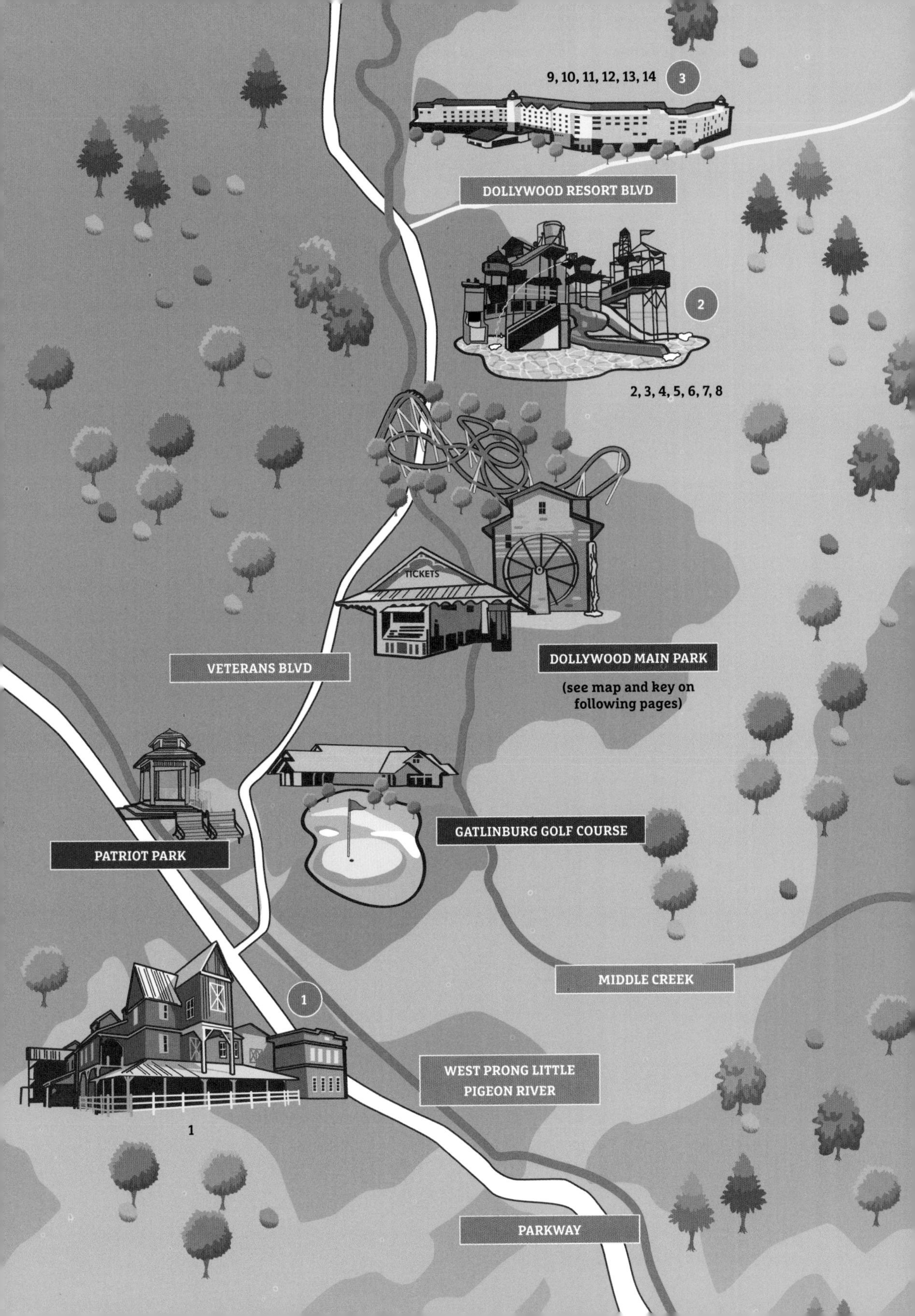
9, 10, 11, 12, 13, 14
3
DOLLYWOOD RESORT BLVD
2
2, 3, 4, 5, 6, 7, 8
TICKETS
VETERANS BLVD
DOLLYWOOD MAIN PARK
(see map and key on following pages)
PATRIOT PARK
GATLINBURG GOLF COURSE
MIDDLE CREEK
1
WEST PRONG LITTLE PIGEON RIVER
1
PARKWAY

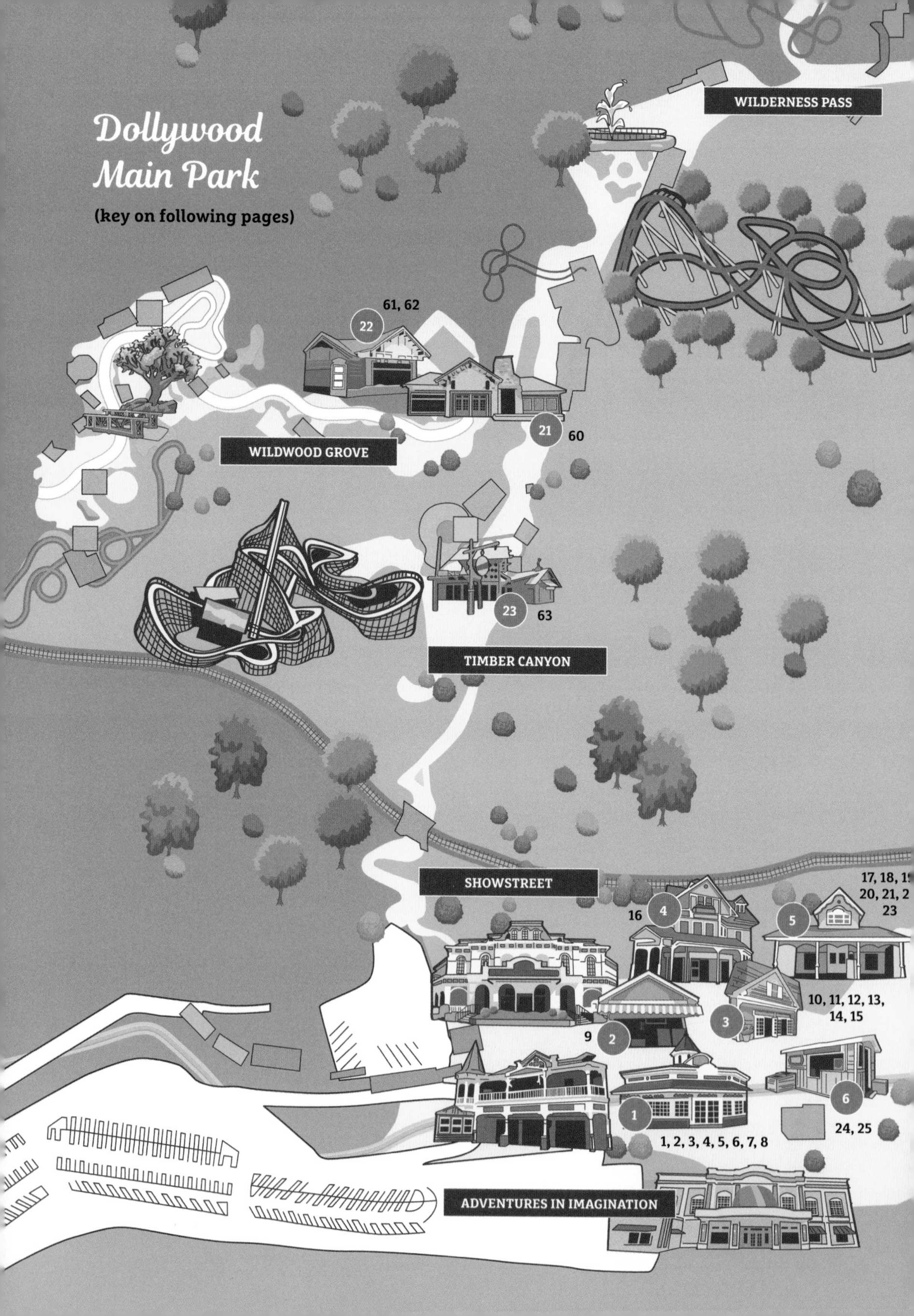

Dollywood
Main Park
(key on following pages)
WILDERNESS PASS
61, 62
22
21
60
WILDWOOD GROVE
23
63
TIMBER CANYON
SHOWSTREET
16
4
5
17, 18,
20, 21,
23
10, 11, 12, 13,
14, 15
9
2
3
6
1
24, 25
1, 2, 3, 4, 5, 6, 7, 8
ADVENTURES IN IMAGINATION

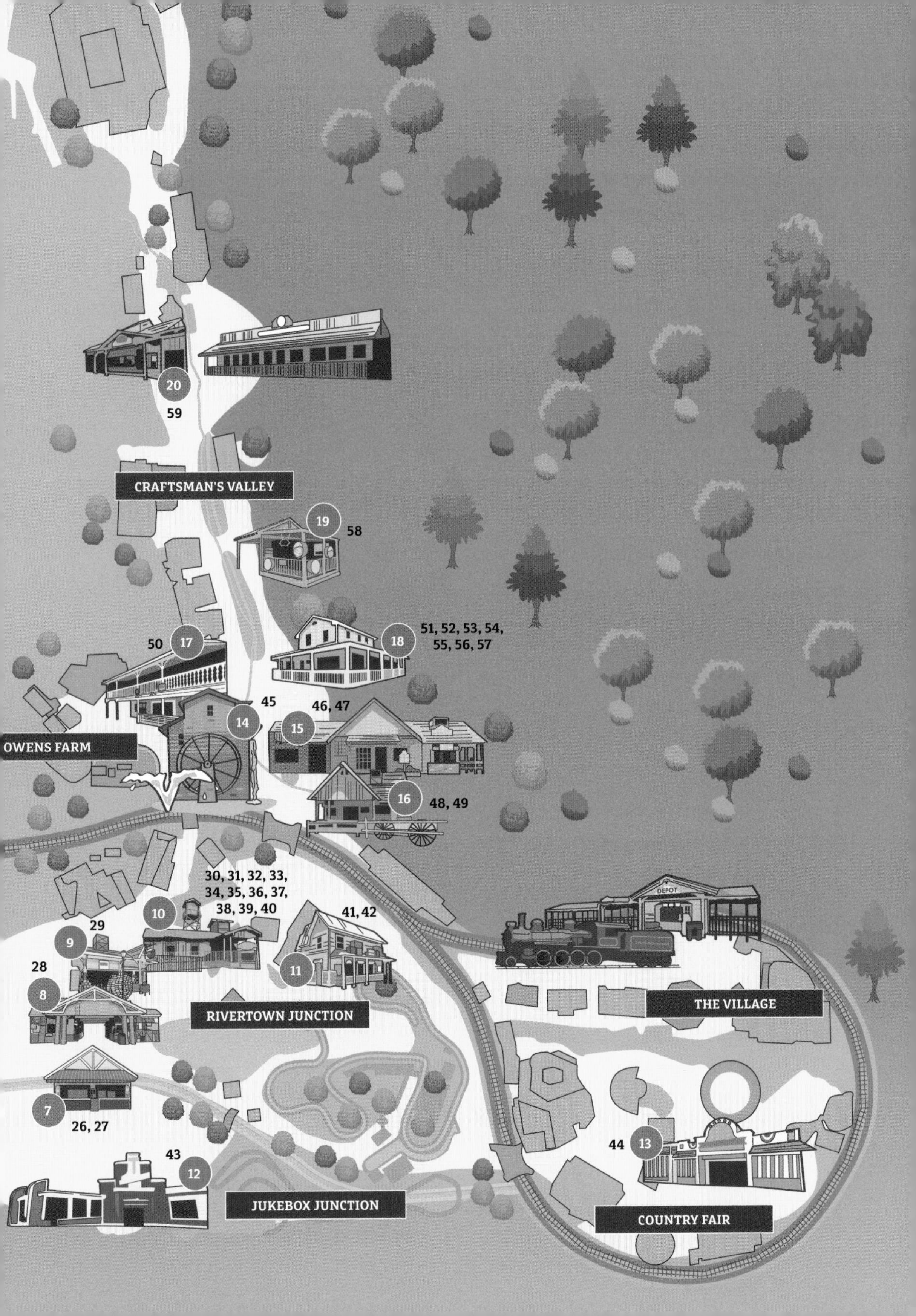

20
59
CRAFTSMAN'S VALLEY
19
58
51, 52, 53, 54,
55, 56, 57
18
50
17
45
14
46, 47
15
OWENS FARM
16
48, 49
30, 31, 32, 33,
34, 35, 36, 37,
38, 39, 40
10
41, 42
DEPOT
29
9
11
28
8
RIVERTOWN JUNCTION
THE VILLAGE
7
26, 27
44
13
43
12
JUKEBOX JUNCTION
COUNTRY FAIR

Showstreet

❶ Spotlight Bakery

❷ Showstreet Frozen Lemonade

❸ Sweet Shoppe Candy Kitchen

❹ Showstreet Ice Cream

❺ Front Porch Café

❻ Showstreet Snacks

Rivertown Junction

❼ Crossroads Funnel Cakes

❽ Market Square BIG SKILLETS®

❾ Country Cookers

❿ Aunt Granny's Restaurant

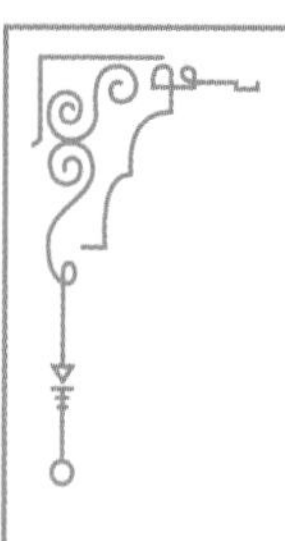

Standard US/Metric Measurement Conversions

VOLUME CONVERSIONS	
US Volume Measure	**Metric Equivalent**
⅛ teaspoon	0.5 milliliter
¼ teaspoon	1 milliliter
½ teaspoon	2 milliliters
1 teaspoon	5 milliliters
½ tablespoon	7 milliliters
1 tablespoon (3 teaspoons)	15 milliliters
2 tablespoons (1 fluid ounce)	30 milliliters
¼ cup (4 tablespoons)	60 milliliters
⅓ cup	90 milliliters
½ cup (4 fluid ounces)	125 milliliters
⅔ cup	160 milliliters
¾ cup (6 fluid ounces)	180 milliliters
1 cup (16 tablespoons)	250 milliliters
1 pint (2 cups)	500 milliliters
1 quart (4 cups)	1 liter (about)
WEIGHT CONVERSIONS	
US Weight Measure	**Metric Equivalent**
½ ounce	15 grams
1 ounce	30 grams
2 ounces	60 grams
3 ounces	85 grams
¼ pound (4 ounces)	115 grams
½ pound (8 ounces)	225 grams
¾ pound (12 ounces)	340 grams
1 pound (16 ounces)	454 grams

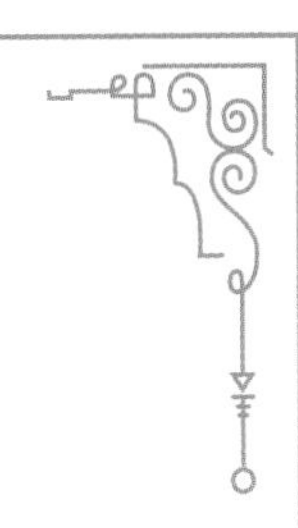

OVEN TEMPERATURE CONVERSIONS	
Degrees Fahrenheit	**Degrees Celsius**
200 degrees F	95 degrees C
250 degrees F	120 degrees C
275 degrees F	135 degrees C
300 degrees F	150 degrees C
325 degrees F	160 degrees C
350 degrees F	180 degrees C
375 degrees F	190 degrees C
400 degrees F	205 degrees C
425 degrees F	220 degrees C
450 degrees F	230 degrees C

BAKING PAN SIZES	
American	**Metric**
8 × 1½ inch round baking pan	20 × 4 cm cake tin
9 × 1½ inch round baking pan	23 × 3.5 cm cake tin
11 × 7 × 1½ inch baking pan	28 × 18 × 4 cm baking tin
13 × 9 × 2 inch baking pan	30 × 20 × 5 cm baking tin
2 quart rectangular baking dish	30 × 20 × 3 cm baking tin
15 × 10 × 2 inch baking pan	30 × 25 × 2 cm baking tin (Swiss roll tin)
9 inch pie plate	22 × 4 or 23 × 4 cm pie plate
7 or 8 inch springform pan	18 or 20 cm springform or loose bottom cake tin
9 × 5 × 3 inch loaf pan	23 × 13 × 7 cm or 2 lb narrow loaf or pâté tin
1½ quart casserole	1.5 liter casserole
2 quart casserole	2 liter casserole

General Index

Note: Page numbers in **bold** indicate recipe category lists.

Index of Recipes in Park Order

Note: The following recipes are featured in the order in which they appear in Dollywood.

About the Author

Erin K. Browne is the blogger and photographer behind *Brownie Bites*, where she shares approachable, easy recipes that are as fun to make as they are to eat. She especially loves pop culture and fandom-inspired recipes, with Dollywood being a major source of such inspiration, as the park is just a short drive from her home. Outside of the kitchen, Erin enjoys reading in a cozy chair, hiking in the mountains, and exploring the country in her family's RV. She currently lives in Knoxville, Tennessee, with her husband, Matt; her two children, Jasper and Shelby; her goofball corgi, Dewey; and the sweetest kitty who ever lived, Ham. Learn more at BrownieBites.net or follow Erin on *Instagram* at @ebrowniebites.